A Brief History of Encyclopaedias

A Brief History of Encyclopaedias

From Pliny to Wikipedia

Andrew Brown

Brief Histories
Published by Hesperus Press Limited
19 Bulstrode Street, London W1U 2JN
www.hesperuspress.com

Designed and typeset by Fraser Muggeridge studio
Printed and bound by CPI Group (UK) Ltd, Croydon CR0 4YY

ISBN: 978-1-84391-973-5

Contents

Introduction

I may not be the best person to write a history of encyclopaedias, however brief. I have never read one. Not all the way through. I greatly admire those who *do* read all the way through an encyclopaedia. They are often unfairly maligned. Sartre's autodidact, in *Nausea*, is engaged in reading the encyclopaedia from A to Z; he is a humanist, who loves mankind (especially young boys) and believes that his universal philanthropy will be bolstered by encyclopaedic knowledge. The text of *Nausea* (in the form of the diary of Roquentin, a jaded historical student on the verge of a nervous breakdown) satirises the autodidact, though not without sympathy. Many years later, in his autobiographical *Words*, Sartre revealed that as a young boy he too had loved encyclopaedias – and that for all the dialectical sophistication of his later philosophising, and for all his rejection of his bourgeois upbringing ('I loathe my childhood and all that remains of it'), he was still, in all important respects, that same young boy.

Though I have never read an encyclopaedia, I have of course read *from* many of them, and still do. Even the most trivial, out-of-date encyclopaedia, bought at a charity shop or jumble sale (where they often languish) can be an object of instruction, amusement, or a yawn of recognition that can at any moment modulate into the slack-jawed gawp of amazement and even a certain degree of awe ('how interesting! how interesting that they thought *that*! how interesting that such a factoid should be deemed of interest – and to whom?').

In the modern world, encyclopaedias (restricting the discussion, just for the moment, to general encyclopaedias) are surrounded by a strange, twilit aura. They are respected as clear and reliable sources of knowledge, but there is something greyly utilitarian in their often workaday prose. The 'circle of knowledge' is ambiguous: a satisfying image of completeness, or a suffocating symbol of closure and futility. They are written by experts and consulted by amateurs, or by schoolchildren doing their homework. Unless it is to grouse, how often will an expert on Ming vases consult the article on that subject in a general encyclopaedia? Encyclopaedias are (like Nietzsche's *Zarathustra*) books for everybody and for nobody. They boast of the number of entries they contain, but usually, the more entries (or 'headwords'), the smaller the entries and the greater the fragmentation. They pride themselves on being up to date, but they become obsolete more rapidly than the weather forecast. No other cultural edifice is simultaneously so monumental and so fragile. An encyclopaedia is 'all you need to know', and yet any encyclopaedia worth its name will constantly undermine this claim to self-sufficiency, referring outwards, either internally ('see also' – the cross-references that remind you that every individual article is a fragment) or externally (in the form of a bibliography). The circle of knowledge soon turns into a spiral, with a considerable centrifugal torque. Stylistically, they tend to a certain monotony, a dryness of exposition and a sobriety of enumeration, which I have dutifully mimicked.

The following short investigation of this strange genre is divided into a historical survey and a brief list of themes that run through encyclopaedias of all times and cultures. In this way I fail to solve, in the same way that encyclopaedias inevitably fail to solve, the tension between historical coherence (which requires linear or logical exposition) and ease of reference (for which alphabetical order is the default setting in almost all encyclopaedias of post-mediaeval times).

Part I
Europe and the West

Antiquity

The Greeks did not have a word for it. 'Encyclopaedia' is a sixteenth-century back-formation – a belated addition to the lexicon of Western thought. The Greeks did, however, have a word for 'busybody'. Socrates was a busybody who interested himself too much in the knowledge of others (or what they claimed to be knowledge) while abstaining from claiming that he had any knowledge of his own to impart. As Diderot was to do 2,000 years later, Socrates went around cross-questioning people on their everyday activities: in particular, on their trades. But whereas Diderot was concerned essentially to report ('How do you make a shoe?') so as to include information in his *Encyclopédie*, Socrates was intent on evaluation ('How do you make a good shoe? What makes a good shoe? Are you a good cobbler? So what?'). In Plato's *Apology*, being a busybody is one of the accusations brought against him by the Athenians: *periergazetai* ('He goes around asking questions') – or, in full: 'Socrates is a criminal and a busybody, investigating the things beneath the earth and in the heavens.'

The younger Socrates does seem to have shown some interest in knowing about the furniture of the world, or cosmology:

> When I was young, Cebes, I was tremendously eager for the kind of wisdom [*sophia*] which they call investigation of nature [*peri phuseos historian* – what eventually became our 'physics']. I thought it was a glorious thing to know the causes of everything, why each thing comes into being and why it perishes and why it exists; and I was always unsettling myself with such questions as these: Do heat and cold, by a sort of fermentation, bring about the organisation of animals, as some people say? Is it the blood, or air, or fire by which we think? Or is it none of these, and does the brain furnish the sensations of hearing and sight and smell, and do memory and opinion arise from these, and does knowledge come from memory and opinion in a state of rest? And again I tried to find out how these things perish, and I investigated the phenomena of heaven and earth until finally I made up my mind that I was by nature totally unfitted for this kind of investigation.
>
> – *Phaedo*

For, having shown an interest in this encyclopaedic range of questions, Socrates then shifted his focus to the nature of the knower: 'I am not yet able, as the Delphic inscription has it, to know myself; so it seems to me ridiculous, when I do not yet know that, to investigate irrelevant things.'

The mature Socrates set himself against the Sophists, who were in a sense the original encyclopaedists – they could teach anything to anybody, at a price. Although the charge of being an intellectual busybody stuck, Socrates turned away from the view of knowledge as essentially a matter of accumulating facts about the world. As Socrates admits at his trial, Aristophanes' comedy *The Clouds* depicts him as uttering all kinds of nonsense – but these are things 'about which I know nothing, either much or little. And I say this, not to cast dishonour about such knowledge, if anyone is wise about such matters…' *If* anyone is wise. Socrates knows he does not know; here, he does not know whether other people do. In this way he performs service to the god: by viewing the knowledge of others sceptically.

How did Socrates' main heirs, Plato and then Aristotle, view the accumulation of knowledge? Jaeger insisted that Plato, unlike Aristotle, was not encyclopaedic. On Plato he wrote: 'The notion of a systematic unity of all sciences was totally foreign to him, and still more so was its realization in an encyclopaedic organization of all subjects for purposes of teaching and research.' And: 'There is nothing to which Plato right down to the end of his life was more passionately opposed than the statement that the soul can know what is just without *being* just' (*see* Ep. VII 344A). To know something involves – or should – the transformation of the knower. And yet, in the *Laws* VII 817E, Plato (or his spokesman) lists the disciplines that should be studied by every free man – a miniature 'educational encyclopaedia' of the kind that recurs throughout European history, since it raises the questions of what can be (and what should be) known. Plato was also interested in the encyclopaedic problems of classification. The Stranger in *The Statesman* says that we should strive to see the common qualities shared by things and also the differences between them insofar as they exist 'in classes' (*en eidesi*). And we need, when faced with dissimilar things, to subsume all those which are related into some class, 'on the basis of their essential nature' – to gather them 'into one circle of similarity'. This is the basis for the Platonic method of division and collection, and the 'circle' of knowledge found in an encyclopaedia would often rely – right up to the end of the Middle Ages, when alphabetical order started to predominate – on classes of *similia*. Admittedly, some of the examples provided in this dialogue of Plato's sound like riddles: what is 'made with wet and dry materials' and 'wrought by fire and without fire'? Answer: the class of receptacles. Which class can be described like this: it is found 'on land and in water, it wanders about and is stationary, it is honourable and without honour, but it has one name, because the whole class is always a seat for some one and exists to be sat upon'? Answer: the class of vehicles. The Stranger admittedly seems to have a sense of humour, but the problems of classification cast their shadow over many encyclopaedic endeavours.

For Aristotle, the universe is a plurality of individual entities (*ex adiaireton ara ton pan* – *Physics* 186b). But it is also divided into different classes of entities: Aristotle was even more fascinated by taxonomy than Plato, and by the different fields of inquiry under which entities fell. The very titles of his books (or rather of his lecture notes, as assembled into 'individual entities' by his students) establish the disciplines which still guide research: physics, metaphysics, ethics, aesthetics (or 'poetics'), meteorology. The research centre (Lyceum) which he founded promoted work in all of these domains. It also showed a propensity towards drawing up lists. Aristotle was a collector – of animals and proverbs (for a collection of which he laid down the foundations). He himself, in collaboration with Callisthenes, embarked on setting down a complete list of the winners of the Pythian Games that was, in the course of several years, duly chiselled in some 60,000 words. It is now lost, as are the results of research into the competitions at the Dionysiac and Lenaean festivals. ('Ah, those Greeks! They always wanted to be *first!*' said Nietzsche.) It is easy to imagine a present-day Aristotle as a bar-room bore, or editing the *Guinness Book of Records*.

The Lyceum, in some ways the first university in the West, or at least in Greece, was highly organised and self-conscious about its own place in the development of the sciences. Aristotle would often begin an investigation into some field of being by concentrating on *ta phainomena*, the way that being manifested itself within that field. It showed itself, for instance, in people's opinions about it (*ta endoxa*), in what had been, and could be, said about it (*ta legomena*).The Lyceum duly produced a series of histories of the different branches of being and thinking: the history of a discipline is a part of that discipline, and the compilation of previous ideas is itself a contribution to their ongoing life. Such activities clearly embodied an encyclopaedic urge: find out what has been done, so as to add to and correct it.

Distinctions between Plato and Aristotle are permeable. The *doxa* has it that Plato is more inclined to mathematics (and distrustful of the defects of the everyday language on which encyclopaedic compilers rely), obsessed by the intimation that an encounter with *the really real* involves a wrench, a conversion, the blinding emergence from the cave, something akin to falling in love, and an endless ascent to the contemplation of the Form of the Good. Aristotle counts more on the teamwork of researchers, patiently sorting through the universe, setting limits, drawing distinctions, inventorying and classifying. 'Platonic' is an adjective we apply to majestically abstract solids, and to an intense sublimatory love; Aristotle has given his name to a certain catfish, *Parasilurus aristotelis*. But the Aristotelian school was driven by the idea that one mind, or the mind, or mind, could grasp the whole of totality in a systematic and interrelated sweep: all encyclopaedias in the West stand in the shadow of this magisterial idea.

Knowledge continued to accumulate, to be recorded in ever vaster compilations; moralists continued to wonder whether true value could be attributed to such knowledge. The tension between knowing things in an organised and methodical way, and knowing lots of things that did not necessarily hang together, persisted throughout antiquity. Plutarch wrote a whole essay 'On Being a Busybody' in which he lambasted *polypragmosune*, and cited Oedipus as an example of unhealthy curiosity. And in 'On Listening to Lectures', he described 'a habit of mind bent on acquiring mere information': *historiken hexin*.

Marcus Porcius Cato's ideal was the good man (*vir bonus*, an echo of the Greek *kalos kagathos*), and he focused on how to live. What to know was subordinate to this aim. Hellenophile Romans were too easily seduced by Greek theory: he composed treatises on such practical matters as oratory, that Roman discipline *par excellence*, and on agriculture, medicine, civil law, and military discipline. Like any good *paterfamilias* he intended to pass on his patrimony to his son, composing the *Praecepta ad Filium* (*Advice to a Son*), telling him to beware Greeks bearing medical certificates.

> In due course, my son Marcus, I shall explain what I found out in Athens about these Greeks, and demonstrate what advantage there may be in looking into their writings (while not taking them too seriously). They are a worthless and unruly tribe. Take this as a prophecy: when those folk give us their writings they will corrupt everything. All the more if they send their doctors here. They have sworn to kill all barbarians with medicine – and they charge a fee for doing it, in order to be trusted and to work more easily. They call us barbarians, too, of course, and *Opici*, a dirtier name than the rest. I have forbidden you to deal with doctors.
>
> – Quoted by Pliny the Elder (*Naturalis Historia*, 29, 13–14)

Not for Cato the over-educated Greek sophisticate, the 'cultivated man' or *pepaideumenos* ('the one-who-has-been-educated' – Berthold Brecht would decide there was something distastefully passive in the German word for 'scholar', *Gelehrte*, which means the same as the Greek word). He ordered the sewers to be cleaned and the aqueducts repaired; he was horrified by the vogue for Bacchanalian mysteries and Greek philosophy, and fought against financial freedom for women. Cato's *De Agri Cultura* (*On Farming*) – the oldest complete prose work in Latin to have survived – advised on husbandry (grape vines, olive harvests, livestock), making a farm profitable, and the treatment of slaves (reduce their rations if they fall ill): an encyclopaedic range of rural interests.

Roman writers of an encyclopaedic bent initially spread their learning over several works. But as the values of traditional Roman society came under increasing attack, especially in the period of the Civil War and the Augustan Principate, there was an increasing need for individual summaries of what was known, what had been thought and believed hitherto – and what was perhaps in danger of being lost. The *De verborum significatu* (*On the Meaning of Words*) of the Augustan grammarian Marcus Verrius Flaccus is an example: it enumerated the customs, myths and beliefs, the gods and monuments, the language and institutions of Italy.

Of Posidonius of Rhodes only fragments and book titles remain. We know that he travelled widely and described the peoples that he encountered, and that he enjoyed a reputation as a polymath, writing on physics, astronomy, divination, geology, seismology, hydrology, botany and other branches of the natural sciences, as well as on mathematics and logic, and anthropology, ethics and history. These subject areas were divided into physics (including metaphysics and theology), logic, and ethics, all brought into a living whole, the Stoic cosmos. Separate things were organically interconnected by *sumpatheia*. From the fragments of his work that remain we have some inkling of an encyclopaedic endeavour carried out in the days of Republican Rome.

Cicero's main focus was on speech and the making of speeches. He encourages the idea of encyclopaedic knowledge as something that exists to be *used*: more specifically to be drawn on in spoken discourse – for the Romans, speech could be a most powerful act. Someone says something: you recognise what they are talking about (or learn it on the spot), and you are able to reply, to hold your end up, to keep the conversation going – in a court of law, to add, embellish, question, or refute. In *De Oratore* III 72 he says that the good orator, as well as possessing the techniques essential to his trade, must be a philosopher in that he must know 'everything'. History is good as a source of concrete examples; philosophy will enable you to distinguish between good and evil, true and false; even astronomy, maths and poetry could be called upon in the courts of law. Think how much a lawyer needs to know (or find out), not just about the law – the constitution, if written, what is legal and what is not, which previous cases provide suitable precedent – but about 'everything': the behaviour to be expected of a heroin addict, the summer timetables of night buses in Saint-Germain-en-Laye, the way viscose shreds, the sewerage system of a particular township in South Africa. So much 'general' knowledge is forensic: the world is the scene of a crime.

Varro, appointed by Julius Caesar as head of the public library in Rome in 47 BC, studied at Athens and was a voluminous writer – more inclined to antiquarianism than to the natural sciences. His *Antiquitatum Rerum Humanorum et Divinarum libri XLI* (*The Antiquity of Things Human and Divine in Forty-One Books*) cover things human (twenty-five of them) and divine (sixteen). Here is a breakdown of his work:

Things Human:
Book 1: Introduction.
Books 2–7: Human beings.
Books 8–13: Places (Rome and Italy; the rest of Europe; Asia and Africa).
Books 14–19: Times (centuries; *lustra*; years; months; days).
Books 20–25: Things.

Things Divine:
Book 26: Introduction.
Books 27–29: Human beings.
Books 30–32: Places.
Books 33–35: Times.
Books 36–38: Things.
Books 38–41: Gods and goddesses.

We know this organisation from Saint Augustine, though the work itself is lost. Even when discussing geography, Varro was concerned mainly to clarify allusions to place-names in the poets. His *Nine Books of Disciplines* formed essentially an encyclopaedia of education. The work focused on the nine arts of grammar, dialectic, rhetoric, geometry, arithmetic, astrology (or astronomy), music, medicine and architecture. Shorn of these last two, the list yielded the seven 'liberal arts', what the Middle Ages would call the 'trivium' (the first three) and the 'quadrivium' (the rest).

One of the last works of Seneca the Younger, before he was ordered by his ungrateful tutee Nero to commit suicide, was the seven-book *Naturales quaestiones* (*Natural Questions*) which largely pillaged previous writers for details of storms and sundogs, meteors, earthquakes, comets, snow, and the sources of the Nile. It also included more specifically practical issues, such as plumbing, and the use of hypocausts in baths. In Stoic fashion, such information about the physical world was deemed to be a basis for ethical considerations.

Pliny the Elder, the author of the *Naturalis historia* (*Natural History*), did little personal research and carried out no experiments. He was drawn to wonders (*mirabilia*). He piled tradition upon hearsay, and legend upon traveller's tale. He sensed that most of the things we know, we know by report: whether this can be said to be true knowledge was not a question that bothered him unduly.

Saint Augustine lived to see Rome sacked by the Goths in AD 410. His *De doctrina Christiana (On Christian Doctrine)* and his *De civitate Dei (City of God)* are both encyclopaedic. The first provides an outline of Christian education: what the believer needed to know (apart, that is, from 'God and the soul'). The second is a kind of negative encyclopaedia: a compilation of all the things that not only do not need to be known, but which, if believed, can lead to disaster. From his time until at least the seventeenth century, all encyclopaedic works in Europe would be essentially religious (Christian, Jewish or Muslim) in their presuppositions. For example, many works of encyclopaedic compendiousness were devoted to the cataloguing of heresies, on the basis *know your enemy*. It is indeed thanks to these works that we still have a large amount of information on such detestable errors, since the religious authorities in power energetically suppressed them. Heresy, crowned with the mitre of reversed flames, took paradoxical shelter in the works that denounced it (an example of the return of the repressed). In Constantinople, in the early twelfth century AD, Euthymios Zigabenus composed his *Dogmatika Panoplia* (*The Panoply of Dogma*), an enormous encyclopaedia of such heresies together with an interpretation of their purport.

The Middle Ages

Cassiodorus (c.485–c.585) worked in the administration of Ostrogothic king Theodoric and by 526, at the time of Theodoric's death, was the head of the civil service. Soon after 540 he retired, and founded the aptly named monastery of Vivarium, near Scylletium, his birthplace. Here he lived for the rest of his life, sheltered from the turbulence of the outside world, still compiling the work of earlier grammarians at the age of 93. He was crucial in the collecting and collating of manuscripts, and wanted to save as many pagan works as possible, for the good of the Christian Church. He wrote, as he put it, 'for the instruction of simple and unpolished brothers': one of his works was a history of the world from Creation up to his own day (the *Chronicon* of 519). His most influential book was the *Institutiones divinarum et saecularum litterarum* (*Institutes of Divine and Secular Literature*), and in its second part it discussed the seven liberal arts in what was, in effect, an encyclopaedia that had wide impact on the culture of the Middle Ages.

Rabanus Maurus (or Hrabanus – his name is cognate with Old German *hraban* or 'raven') lived from c.780–856, and was abbot of Fulda and archbishop of Mainz (his home town); he was a Benedictine who studied with Alcuin at Tours. He enjoyed a reputation as the most learned man of his age. His most encyclopaedic work is the *De rerum naturis* or *De universo*, comprising twenty-two books written in the 840s. Like many such compilations, it was an aid for preachers, divided by subject area, from Book 1 (God and the angels), to Book 22 (months, food, vessels, and instruments used in fields and gardens and in the tending of horses). Book 8 is a bestiary, with discussions of lions, tigers, panthers, pards, the 'rhinoceros' (monocerus and unicorn), elephants, griffins, chameleons, lynxes, 'hydruses' (hydras) and dragons, hedgehogs, ants and frogs, salamanders and sea snakes.

In the work of Isidore, bishop of Seville from c.600, we find something of a linguistic turn in the area of encyclopaedias. He was renowned for his learning: his pupil Braulio, bishop of Saragossa, wrote: 'In him antiquity reasserted itself – or rather, our time laid in him a picture of the wisdom of antiquity: a man practised in every form of speech, he adapted himself in the quality of his words to the ignorant and the learned, and was distinguished for unequalled eloquence when there was fit opportunity.' Isidore chaired the fourth Council of Toledo (633), which united Church and State, and decreed toleration of Jews (in spite of Isidore's own *Contra Judaeos*); he continued the heroic work of his brother Leander, bishop of Seville before him, in converting the Visigoths from Arianism (the doctrine teaching that the Son was not equal to the Father, nor eternal) to Catholicism; he is now in Paradise (*see* Dante).

Isidore of Seville wrote voluminously: the one-book *De Rerum Natura* (*On the Nature of Things*) was a description of the universe dedicated to the Visigoth king Sisebut, 'in which he cleared up certain obscurities about the elements by studying the works of the Church Fathers as well as those of the philosophers' (Braulio); the *Chronica* was a history of the world; the *De Ordine Creaturarum* (*On the Order of Creatures*) surveyed both the material and the spiritual dimensions of the whole of reality. Isidore's most encyclopaedic work, however, was the *Etymologiarum sive originum libri XX* (*Twenty Books on Origins or Etymologies*), commonly known as the *Etymologiae*. Braulio calls it:

> a vast work which [Isidore] left unfinished, and which I have divided into twenty books, since he wrote it at my request. And whoever meditatively reads this work, which is in every way profitable for wisdom, will not be ignorant of human and divine matters. There is an exceeding elegance in his treatment of the different arts in this work in which he has gathered well-nigh everything that ought to be known.

It drew on Pliny the Elder, Solinus, Aristotle, Justinius, Lucretius, Cassiodorus, Servius, Suetonius, Hyginus, Ambrose, Augustine, Orosius, Tertullian, Sallust, Hegesippus, et al. Isidore was vastly hospitable to pagan learning: such a liberal attitude would become rare in the High Middle Ages.

Isidore was not interested, unlike us moderns, in criticising his sources. He has been criticised for his complaisant use of out-of-date information. He repeats the anecdotes of his forebears (who themselves had largely quoted each other), knowing that truth did not essentially lie in the correspondence between text and world. His title, *Etymologiae*, shows that for Isidore, reality was to be approached through language – and through the essence of language, its origin, for it is a profoundly Cratylean work. In twenty volumes, it covers grammar (Book 1), rhetoric and logic (Book 2), arithmetic, geometry, music, astronomy (Book 3), medicine (Book 4), law and chronology (Book 5), theology (Books 6–8), the human body (Book 11), zoology (Book 12), cosmography and physical geography (Books 13–14), architecture and surveying (Book 15 and part of Book 19), mineralogy (Book 16), agriculture (Book 17), military science (Book 18), ships and building (Book 19), and 'victuals and domestic and agricultural instruments' (Book 20). But all of these topics are brought under the sway of the signifier. Isidore knew that the 'true' names of all things (their *etyma*) were those they bore in the 'first' language, Hebrew – a meaning that had subsequently been concealed and could be recovered (though his own etymologies are mainly in Latin, with some use of Greek). He wrote:

> A knowledge of etymology is often necessary in interpretation, for, when you see whence a name has come, you grasp its force more quickly. For every consideration of a thing is clearer when its etymology is known. Not all names, however, were given by the ancients in accordance with nature, but certain also according to whim, just as we sometimes give slaves and estates names according to our fancy.

He was guided by the shape and sound of words rather than by the etymologies that are nowadays recognised. 'Bees [Latin *apes*] are so called either because they bind themselves together with their feet [Latin *pes*] or because they are born without feet [a Greek negative particle + Latin *pes* – *a-pes*]' (tr. Grant). 'The eagle [Latin *aquila*] is so called from its sharpness [Latin *acumen*] of sight' (tr. Brehaut). But here, to give an idea of the way Isidore links etymologies to broader information about the world, is a longer excerpt:

> The knees are the meeting-points of the thighs and lower legs; and they are called knees (*genua*) because in the womb they are opposite to the cheeks (*genae*). For they adhere to them there and they are akin to the eyes, the revealers of tears and of pity. [...] *Lac* (milk) derives its name from its colour, because it is a white liquor, for the Greeks call white λεῦκος and its nature is changed from blood; for after the birth whatever blood has not yet been spent in the nourishing of the womb flows by a natural passage to the breasts, and whitening by their virtue, receives the quality of milk.
>
> 86. *Ossa* (bones) are the solid parts of the body. For on these all form and strength depend. *Ossa* are named from *ustus* (burned), because they were burned by the ancients, or as others think, from *os* (the mouth), because there they are visible, for everywhere else they are covered and concealed by the skin and flesh.

> 92. *Mus* (mouse) is a tiny animal; it has a Greek name; but any word that is derived from it becomes Latin. Others say *mures* are so named because they are born from the *humor* (moisture) of the earth. […] The liver of these creatures grows at the full moon, just as certain things that belong to the sea grow, which grow smaller again when the moon lessens.

It is in Book 12 of his *Etymologiae* that Isidore focuses most on animals: he largely underplays the allegorising of earlier writers, though this would be taken up by later compilers of bestiaries. So the *Aberdeen Bestiary* (f. 37v) claims to be repeating Isidore, but is in fact attributing to him moral meanings that are not there in the *Etymologiae*:

> In his book of Etymologies, Isidore says that the raven picks out the eyes in corpses first, as the Devil destroys the capacity for judgement in carnal men, and proceeds to extract the brain through the eye. The raven extracts the brain through the eye, as the Devil, when it has destroyed our capacity for judgement, destroys our mental faculties.

Another bestiary, by Philippe de Thaon, quotes Isidore on the ant: 'Isidore speaks of the ant in his writing, and shows the reason well why it is named formica. It is *fortis* (strong), and carries *mica* (a particle), that is the meaning of the name; there is no creature of so small a shape, which carries by its own force so great a burden…' (tr. Wright).

Isidore Ducasse (1846–70) was named after Isidore of Seville, and adopted the nom de plume of the Comte de Lautréamont, whose name signifies 'other', 'author', and 'uphill' – his *Chants de Maldoror*, written about the same time as the Commune de Paris (1871), is an anti-encylopaedic work in which creation has come adrift from its divine underpinnings and categories collapse into one another – a world without what modern philosophers call 'natural kinds'. But in odd respects, Ducasse's namesake and forebear had also transgressed the boundaries between one discreet thing and another since he believed in the primacy of the word and its etymological underpinnings.

'Learn everything: later you will see that nothing is useless' ('*omnia disce, videbis postea nihil esse superfluum*'), wrote Hugh of Saint Victor in his *Didascalicon*. This generous attitude was typical of the monks of the Abbey of Saint Victor in Paris: though they aimed mainly at cultivating mystical insight, they thought that knowledge of the world could act as a prolegomenon to this. (Rabelais would later satirise scholastic learning in his parodic list of the books in the Abbey of Saint Victor that were perused by Pantagruel.) Hugh's own mysticism is rather beautifully described (by Ch. V. Langlois) in the eleventh edition of the *Encyclopaedia Britannica* as 'learned, unctuous, ornate, florid, a mysticism which never indulges in dangerous temerities; it is the orthodox mysticism of a subtle and prudent rhetorician'. The *Didascalicon* of Hugh covers the trivium and quadrivium, the theoretical and the practical sciences. The mechanical sciences aim essentially at the relief of the human condition (truth comes from theoretical, and virtue from practical, philosophy): and, after all, both Saint Joseph and Saint Paul were engaged in manual work. His method of exposition was to take an activity, such as the spinning of wool, and then divide it into several sub-activities, each with a list of the requisite tools. An encyclopaedia could now generate itself from a few initial headwords that could be broken down into genera and species, divided and subdivided, thus filling the world with knowable things.

Mediaeval scribes were involved in a gruelling, back-breaking form of manual labour. They would usually be hunkered down on a bench, the parchment perched on their knees; otherwise they stood at a high desk. It was painful work, having to hold a stylus for long periods. They were frequently enjoined to revere the Trinity by using three straight digits, their forefinger, middle finger and thumb, to write, with the front of the arm held upright. But the result of this labour was that mediaeval encyclopaedias could be things of great beauty, and some are as famous for their illustrations as for their texts. Herrad of Landsberg was the abbess of Hohenburg, in the Vosges mountains some fifteen miles outside Strasbourg. She produced a marvellously illuminated manuscript encyclopaedia, the *Hortus deliciarum* (*Garden of Delights*): some 300 folio leaves of parchment, illustrated – and this is its chief claim to fame – with about 9,000 figures in 340 or so miniatures, 130 of them illuminations in colour, historical and allegorical in theme (they depict in particular the battle between Virtue and Vice, and include portraits of her fellow nuns, for whose edification the work was composed: the images are accompanied by explanations in Latin, sometimes glossed in German). Excerpts from ancient writers are accompanied by poems by Herrad herself. Although the illustrations in particular (drawn by several people) were meant for female novices, the work was theologically advanced – it drew both on Anselm and Bernard of Clairvaux, but also on contemporary writers being taught in the schools for young men, such as Peter Lombard and Peter Comestor.

Here is a description of angels from the *Hortus*:

> Concerning the Angels
> All the companies of the angels are named as being spiritual in nature. Moreover, they have received diverse titles based on different duties, namely: seraphim, cherubim, thrones, dominions, sovereigns, powers, virtues, archangels, angels. Those companies of holy beings are called 'seraphim', who, because of their unique nearness to the Maker, burn with incomparable love for Him. For those who burn are called 'seraphim'. Further, cherubim are named due to fullness of knowledge, because they are filled by knowledge to such great perfection as they contemplate in clarity God more closely.

The original manuscript was moved to the Library in Strasbourg at the French Revolution, and destroyed when the library was burned down during the siege of 1870, in the Franco-Prussian War, though a good impression can be gained from copies of it that had by this time been made.

On a more humble note, the *Hortus deliciarum* also contains the first depiction of a pretzel. But many encyclopaedias could still be produced as, essentially, guides to good behaviour. Thus Raoul Ardent wrote a *Speculum universale* that was also known as the *Summa de vitiis et virtutibus* (*Summary of Vices and Virtues*), devoted entirely to theological topics – the redemption, the active versus the contemplative life, the four cardinal virtues, etc. This was all a Christian needed to know.

Gervase of Tilbury (c.1150–c.1220) was from Essex, and a descendant of the fairy Melusine. He had a more down-to-earth approach to knowledge than Raoul, but his work equally has a moral purpose: in this case, Gervase wanted to produce a mirror for princes, and this was a common aspiration of encyclopaedias in the Middle Ages. He travelled widely and was appointed Marshal of the Kingdom of Arles under Emperor Otto IV (who was also born and bred in England). To keep this drowsy emperor awake, he completed, in around 1211, the *Otia imperialia* (*Recreation for an Emperor*, also known comfortingly as the *Solatio imperatoris* or enticingly as the *Liber de mirabilibus mundi* or more objectively as the *Descriptio totius orbis*). It is divided into three parts (*Decisiones*). The first discusses the Creation of the World; fairies; fauns and satyrs; the Flood, and the rainbow that followed it. The rainbow is a sign of two judgements: that of water, which is past, and that of fire, which is still to come. 'That is why it has two colours: blue, which is the colour of water, and is on the outside because it is past; and red, which is the colour of fire, and is on the inside because the fire is still to come' (I.25). (Contrast this with later descriptions of the rainbow, which tend to concentrate on its more physical characteristics – as in Newton – or else re-allegorise it as part of the sufferings of white light, as in Goethe.) Book 2 continues the story: Noah's sons divide the world up between them, so we are treated to an account of this world, together with a topography of the Holy Land. The third book is dedicated to a list of marvels (*mirabilia*). It was partly the tendency of learning to collapse into lists of *mirabilia* that drew the critical attention of church thinkers who were more concerned with doctrine and orthopraxy than with idle *curiositas*. *Mirabilia* encouraged a kind of epistemological gape ('fancy that!') – a kind of 'believe it or not' attitude that contrasted with the 'believe it or else' of the severer clerics. Gervase's marvels included the loadstone, and the salt supply of Droitwich, now celebrated as Droitwich Spa. In 'your grandfather's kingdom', Gervase reminds Otto, from Christmas to Midsummer's Day, Droitwich wells produce very salty water – in fact we now know that it rivals in salinity the Dead Sea – though the rest of the year it is sweet. He also mentions the apples of Pentapolis, which for Gervase were the five Cities of the Plain submerged in the Dead Sea. 'In the land of Sodom apples grow which are very beautiful to look at. They grow in the usual season, and come to full ripeness in due time; but then if they are broken open, they yield only smoke and ashes.' (Translated by S.E. Banks and J.W. Binns.) The ashes are supposed to be those from the destruction of Sodom.

These apples are also mentioned in other sources, including that late Father of the Church, Chateaubriand, who in the first years of the nineteenth century brought some back with him from his travels in the Middle East.

Gervase refers to the fact that the English had special words for 'skylight', 'forester' and 'werewolf'. This, and his reference to Droitwich, shows that he knew his homeland well – whether much of this knowledge was first-hand is uncertain. The devil chose to appear to Eve in the shape of a 'serpent with a woman's face' because 'like approves of like' (*quia similia similibus applaudunt*). 'Women can still change into serpents – a fact that is certainly remarkable, but not to be repudiated. For in England we have often seen [*Vidimus enim frequenter*] men change into wolves according to the phases of the moon. The Gauls call men of this kind *gerulfi*, while the English name for them is *werewolves* [*Angli vero* were wolf *dicunt*], *were* being the English equivalent of *uir* (man).' (This etymology is, according to the best of today's sources, correct.) Gervase goes on to say that the women of Greece and Jerusalem regularly 'turn men who spurn their desire into asses' who then have to bear heavy burdens, though after a suitable time for punishment the women sometimes take pity on them and turn them back into men. (Saint Augustine had referred to Italian landladies who were equally inclined to metamorphose their guests: *Civitas Dei* xviii 18.) Gervase: 'I do not know whether to attribute all this to an optical trick (*delusioni oculorum*) by which witnesses are deceived, or whether it is a result of there being demons at large in the world which suddenly reconstitute the elements of the things we are talking about (which is what Augustine says happened in the case of the rods which the magicians turned into serpents).'

Unusually for an encyclopaedia, the *Otia* contain many stories as well as facts. One concerns a native of Bristol who was once on a long voyage in 'a remote part of the ocean'. One morning, he sat down to eat, at 9 a.m. As he washed his knife at the ship's rail, it suddenly slipped out of his fingers. 'That very hour it fell through an open window in the roof of the citizen's own home – the kind of window which the English call a skylight [*fenestram... quam lucernariam Angli nominant*] – and stuck fast in a table which stood beneath it, before the eyes of his wife.' She kept it, and showed it to her husband when – long afterwards – he returned from his voyage: to their amazement, they calculated that he had dropped the knife on exactly the same day that she had acquired it. 'Who then will doubt, given the manifest proof of this event, that there is a sea situated above the world we live in, in the air or above the air?' (*Otia* I.13, p. 83).

Gervase is also an astute recorder of local folklore, including the Arthurian legend. In Britain, the 'keepers of the woods (whom the people call foresters) [*quos foristarios... uulgus nominat*]' recount that, at noon or after nightfall, by the light of a full moon, they see a band of knights out hunting: the knights, when questioned, say that they are Arthur's (II.12). This is a typical digression, in the context of a long description of Sicily: the text flies off at a tangent because it is told that, 'in our own times', King Arthur has appeared in the dark recesses of Mount Etna, where, taking his ease in a marvellous palace on a 'wide and beautiful plain', Arthur is recovering from the wounds inflicted on him when he fought 'his nephew Mordred, and Chelric, duke of the Saxons'. The tale of the hunting knights in Britain is similar (*consimilia*). Gervase finishes his Arthurian digression with the words: 'Well, having dealt with those things that have a legendary ring about them ['*ad instar fabularum*'], let us return to our subject. It is quite legitimate to ask how there come to be such great fires and earthquakes in Sicily. My answer is that there is an abyss [*abissus*] in the earth, that is, a vast depth, so-called because it is without [*abest*] a bottom' (II.12).

There was a shift, as the Middle Ages progressed, from Latin to the vernacular. Gautier de Metz (more properly, in his native Loherains, Gauthier de Més) flourished in the thirteenth century. The *Image du monde* of c.1245, also known as the *Mappemonde*, has sometimes been attributed to him, sometimes to a Flemish theologian called Gossuin, though a third group of scholars think that these were one and the same person. It is, unusually for an encyclopaedia (that most prosaic of forms), written in French octosyllables. As its name suggests, it is based on the *Imago mundi* by Honorius Inclusus. It gives an account of creation, geography, astronomy, treasures, monsters, and it circulated in many manuscripts and languages, often beautifully illustrated, throughout the Middle Ages.

Mediaeval encyclopaedias could begin with practical affairs and then lift up their eyes to the heavens. But most started with God. Many were composed at the behest of, or appealed to the patronage of, rulers, as we have seen with Cassiodorus and

Isidore and Gervase. Little is known of the life of Vincent of Beauvais, but several of his works were commissioned by royalty. He was lector and chaplain at the court of Louis IX of France. His *Speculum majus* was written for the education of the man who would become Saint Louis; it was completed in 1258 and republished continually after that, as late as 1624. It followed the classification of Hugh of Saint Victor, being divided into three parts: the *Speculum naturale* (God, Creation, mankind); the *Speculum doctrinale* (language, ethics, crafts, medicine) and the *Speculum historiale* (the history of the world). Like Isidore, he drew widely on non-Christian as well as Christian works, insofar as the two sets were in harmony. This was to be the most important encyclopaedia in Europe for centuries. It seems to have been meant more for individual study than for exposition in lectures: a 'teach yourself' book rather than a textbook. It was translated into French (in 1328), it was known to Chaucer, and it was printed in Paris (1495–6, as news of the New World was filtering across Europe). It was well known in the Renaissance (there is a beautiful edition published by Duaci in 1624 by Baltazar Bellerus), and the whole work was still being revised and reissued in 1879. It was a huge panorama of thirteenth-century learning, and showed considerable familiarity with Aristotle, Cicero and Hippocrates.

The *Speculum naturale*, on natural history, is filled with quotations from Latin, Greek, Hebrew and Arabic sources, with the author's own commentaries (signalled by the rubric *Auctor* – like many encyclopaedists, Vincent was concerned to deny that he had added anything too 'original'). Book 1 is on Creation, and takes the form of a commentary on Genesis. The second book speaks of the Creation, of light, of colours, of the four elements and the fall of the rebel angels. We learn whether angels can communicate thought (*Auctor* decides that they can think and speak, and do not rely on thought transference but have their own language). These were the works of the first day. Books 3 and 4 are devoted to the soul and time, and to meteorology (rain, thunder, winds, dew); 5–14 are on the sea and rivers, agriculture, metals, precious stones, and plants (together with any medicinal properties they may possess), largely in alphabetical order. In Book 6 Vincent asks what would happen if a hole were bored right through the earth, and a stone dropped into it. The stone, he decides (correctly) would fall down and down to the centre of the earth. Book 15 is on astronomy and the seasons; books 16–17 on fowl and fish; 18–22 on wild and domestic animals (dogs, snakes, bees, insects); 23–28 on psychology, physiology, and the five senses of human beings, plus their organs, sleep, dreams, ecstasy, memory. The last four add various miscellaneous information, with the last one concentrating on geography and history.

The *Speculum doctrinale* (17 books, 2,374 chapters) may seem doomed, as its title suggests, to being a mere theological compendium. In fact, it is much more exciting – a survey of a whole range of cultural activities: the mechanical arts, military tactics, logic and surgery. Book 1 is on philosophy; books 2–3 on grammar, logic, rhetoric and poetry; Book 3 includes several useful fables ('The Lion and the Mouse'), and books 4–5 discuss virtue. It is Book 6 that is perhaps most multifarious: advice on building houses; gardening; animal breeding; wine-growing, and an almanac for every month. Book 15, curiously, is a kind of summary of the *Speculum naturale*: a mirror within the mirror. The other books include advice for princes (another mirror: what you should be, what you should know, if you are to rule wisely), canon and civil law, trade, hunting and navigation, medicine, mathematics and music.

The *Speculum historiale* offers a resume of the first two *specula* plus a universal history, based on the *Chronicon* by Helinand of Froidmont, organised in accordance with the six ages of the world. When printed in 1627, it covered almost 1,400 big double-column pages. A fourth section, the *Speculum morale*, was added after Vincent's death, so that the *Speculum triplex* became the *Speculum quadruplex* known to the Renaissance. Perhaps an 'ethical' supplement was deemed to be necessary: at all events, the contents of this last part were derived from Aquinas' *Summa theologiae* and a few other writers such as Stephen de Bourbon.

Vincent could write with equal authority on angels and excrement. Book 13, ch. 168, is on urine (Vincent here relies on Rabanus): it discusses its nineteen different colours, its density, its frequency, and its other qualities (wetness or dryness).

Albert the Great, the teacher of Thomas Aquinas, was persuaded to take Holy Orders by the Blessed Virgin Mary, who told the scholastics to read Aristotle – a philosopher in the transmission and explication of whose thought Albert duly played a crucial role (and to whose errors he devoted a long chapter in his *Summa theologica*). He read many other writers, too, and became 'one of the most erudite men of his age' (a recurring theme in these one-man encyclopaedists); his works cover logic, theology, botany, geography, astronomy, astrology, mineralogy, chemistry, zoology, physiology and phrenology, and this was not mere book-learning, for (says the *Catholic Encyclopaedia*) all of his knowledge – whose multifariety earned him the title of 'Doctor Universalis' – was 'the result of logic and observation'. Albert himself says: 'The aim of natural science is not simply to accept the statements [*narrata*] of others, but to investigate the causes that are at work in nature' (*De Miner.*, Book 2, tr. ii, i), and he emphasised the importance of experience (*experimentum*) and the appeal to causes immanent in nature rather than automatic citation of God's power as the explanation for all miracles. So he went on a whale hunt to Friesland and observed Greenland whales. He loved animals and was devoted to falconry. He amassed insects and plants, and collected drawings of them. '*Vidit infinita*', said Roger Bacon of him: 'he saw infinite things'.

Alexander von Humboldt admired Albert's knowledge of physical geography (*Cosmos*, II, vi); Meyer admired his botany as the most profound and vivid between Theophrastus and the Renaissance (Albert stated that several rocks and plants, especially amethysts, could promote clairvoyance).

Albert's most encyclopaedic work was his 1245 *Tractatus de natura boni summa theologica* (*The Theological Summa or Treatise on the Nature of the Good*). Based on a discussion of Aristotle's ethical and scientific works, it covered logic, rhetoric, mathematics, astronomy, economics, politics, ethics and metaphysics.

Indeed, the Dominicans – the main teaching order of the Catholic Church – were particularly active in the making of encyclopaedias. Thomas de Cantimpré (1201–72), or Thomas of Brabant, was one of the canons regular of Saint Augustine in the abbey of Cantimpré and later a Dominican priest, who studied with Albert the Great and was professor of philosophy in Louvain. His vast *Liber de natura rerum* (*Book on the Nature of Things*) was written between 1230–45. It is a compilation of everything of the natural sciences that a priest of his day could be expected to know. The version completed in 1244 was of twenty books:

1. The human body
2. The heart
3. The monstrous human races of the East
4. Animals (quadrupeds)
5. Birds
6. Marine monsters
7. Fish
8. Snakes
9. Worms (insects)
10. Common trees
11. Aromatic (spice) and medicinal trees
12. Properties of the aromatic and medicinal plants (herbal)
13. Authorities and sources
14. Valuable stones (gems)
15. Seven metals
16. Seven celestial areas
17. The spheres of the Earth and seven planets
18. The motion of the air (winds, weather)

19. The four elements
20. Eclipses and celestial motion

This work had wide influence, being translated into German and French. The *Der Naturen Bloeme* of Jacob van Maerlant is an almost exact copy, translated into Flemish/Middle Dutch, with many adaptations. (Maerlant's work is also arranged by theme, though the 'entries' within each chapter are in more or less alphabetical order: as is common with bestiaries of the period, many of the animals Maerlant describes are mythical or at least unknown – some of his sea creatures are transpositions of land animals transposed into a marine environment: sea-cow, sea-stag, sea-dog, sea-horse and sea-pig, which resemble their terrestrial counterparts, but with added fish tails and fins.) Thomas de Cantimpré's own teacher Albert the Great drew on his *Liber de natura rerum* in his *De Animalibus*, as did Bartholomaeus Anglicus in his *De proprietatibus rerum*, and Vincent of Beauvais in his *Speculum naturale*. However, as the thirteenth century progressed, the Dominicans showed an increasing wariness towards the natural sciences, and Thomas shifted his focus to pastoral care.

We have already met one English encyclopaedist, Gervase. Bartholomaeus Anglicus or Bartholomew the Englishman (c.1203–72) came from Suffolk, and studied natural sciences and theology at Oxford under Robert Grosseteste, later bishop of Lincoln, and then went to Paris where he became a Franciscan and taught theology. In the *studium* at Magdeburg, probably in the 1240s, he wrote *De proprietatibus rerum* (*On the Properties of Things*), as a general compendium for 'ordinary people' – his fellow Franciscans. His work covered all the sciences as known at that time, including theology, philosophy, medicine, astronomy, chronology, zoology, botany, geography and mineralogy. Its success is proved by the fact that it was frequently borrowed in the libraries of the University of Paris.

The work is in nineteen books, since nineteen is a universal number (the twelve signs of the zodiac plus the seven planets):

1. God
2. The angels
3. The soul
4. The (four) elements
5. The human body
6. The ages of man and the states of men and women respectively
7. Illnesses
8. The earth and the heavens (including the circles of the heavens, the zodiac, the motions of the planets, sun and moon)
9. Time (the seasons of the year, the hours of the day)
10. Matter and form (including fire and *materia prima*)
11. The air (including weather; wind, clouds, rain, snow, lightning)
12. Birds (with the description of thirty-eight air-dwelling creatures)
13. Water (including wells, pools and rivers; rivers and lakes in the Bible; the ocean)
14. Mountains (especially those mentioned in the Bible)
15. The regions of the world (geography)
16. Stones and metals
17. Herbs and plants
18. Animals (biblical animals; beasts, serpents, domestic animals, insects)
19. Accidentals (the senses; colours; sounds; smells; taste; weight and measures; liquids)

Book 19 is particularly sensuous – bright colours, aromatic scents, mouth-watering flavours, intoxicating liquors. It includes a list of thirty-six eggs. The work was one of the sources (with Isidore of Seville) for the mysterious travelogue of the gouty and perhaps non-existent Sir John Mandeville, his *Voyage and Travels*, and also for Richard Rolle's *The Pricke of Conscience* (c.1348):

encyclopaedias could still inspire travellers (however fictitious) and moralists in equal degree.

Bartholomaeus quotes from Greek, Jewish and Arabic writers who were being translated into Latin throughout this period, and from standard authorities such as Aristotle, Hippocrates, Pliny, Augustine, Boethius, Rabanus Maurus, Solinus, and Isidore of Seville. The *De proprietatibus rerum* was influential for centuries, and widely translated: the English version by John of Trevisa is particularly flavoursome.

It is instructive to see how information was transmitted, with variations, from one encyclopaedia to another. Here is a basilisk as described in several such compilations:

> Anyone who sees the eyes of a basilisk serpent (*basilisci serpentis*) dies immediately. It is no more than twelve inches long, and has white markings on its head that look like a diadem. Unlike other snakes, which flee its hiss, it moves forward with its middle raised high. Its touch and even its breath scorch grass, kill bushes and burst rocks. Its poison is so deadly that once when a man on a horse speared a basilisk, the venom travelled up the spear and killed not only the man, but also the horse. A weasel can kill a basilisk; the serpent is thrown into a hole where a weasel lives, and the stench of the weasel kills the basilisk at the same time as the basilisk kills the weasel.
>
> – Pliny the Elder (*Natural History*, 8, 33)

> The basilisk is six inches in length and has white spots; it is the king (*regulus*) of snakes. All flee from it, for it can kill a man with its smell or even by merely looking at him. Birds flying within sight of the basilisk, no matter how far away they may be, are burned up. Yet the weasel can kill it; for this purpose people put weasels into the holes where the basilisk hides. They are like scorpions in that they follow dry ground and when they come to water they make men

frenzied and hydrophobic. The basilisk is also called *sibilus*, the hissing snake, because it kills with a hiss.

– Isidore of Seville (*Etymologies*, Book 12, 4:6–9)

The cockatrice hight Basiliscus in Greek, and Regulus in Latin; and hath that name Regulus of a little king, for he is king of serpents, and they be afraid, and flee when they see him. For he slayeth them with his smell and with his breath: and slayeth also anything that hath life with breath and with sight. In his sight no fowl nor bird passeth harmless, and though he be far from the fowl, yet it is burned and devoured by his mouth. But he is overcome of the weasel; and men bring the weasel to the cockatrice's den, where he lurketh and is hid. For the father and maker of everything left nothing without remedy… there is also a serpent that is bred in the province of Sirena; and hath a body in length and in breadth as the cockatrice, and a tail of twelve inches long, and hath a speck in his head as a precious stone, and feareth away all serpents with hissing. And he presseth not his body with much bowing, but his course of way is forthright, and goeth in mean. He drieth and burneth leaves and herbs, not only with touch but also by hissing and blast he rotteth and corrupteth all things about him. And he is of so great venom and perilous, that he slayeth and wasteth him that nigheth him by the length of a spear, without tarrying; and yet the weasel taketh and overcometh him, for the biting of the weasel is death to the cockatrice. And nevertheless the biting of the cockatrice is death to the weasel. And that is sooth, but if the weasel eat rue before. And though the cockatrice be venomous without remedy, while he is alive, yet he loseth all the malice when he is burnt to ashes. His ashes be accounted good and profitable in working of Alchemy, and namely in turning and changing of metals.

– Bartholomaeus Anglicus (*De proprietatibus rerum*, Book 18, in the Trevisa translation)

Most encyclopaedias, as we have seen, were by and for clerks. But not all. Brunetto Latini (c.1220–94), a Guelph of Florence, went into exile in France after the defeat of the Guelphs at the Battle of Montaperti in 1260. He returned in 1266, and became a celebrated teacher. Giovanni Villani the historian says that Brunetto was the 'initiator and master in refining the Florentines and in teaching them how to speak well, and how to guide our republic according to political philosophy [*la politica*]'. He became the intellectual guru of a whole generation of poets and politicians. In France, he had composed *Li livres dou tresor* (c.1266), breaking through to a more bourgeois audience. It was very popular: editions of it were still coming out in the 1530s. He also wrote a short version of it in Italian, the *Tesoretto*, and it was translated into the French of France (rather than of Provence) as *Le trésor qui parle de toutes choses* (*The Treasure that Speaks of all Things*). Dante was Brunetto's pupil: he learned a great deal from his teacher's treasure, though he condemns Brunetto to the circle of the sodomites in the Inferno, in an episode that combines affection, respect, and a grim settling of accounts. (It has been claimed that Dante condemned Brunetto less for the vice of clerks than for writing in French rather than in his own native language of Tuscan – but encyclopaedias were often in any case translated or adapted into other languages.) Napoleon was a great admirer of Brunetto, and intended that the French text of the *Tesoro* be printed with commentaries: he even appointed a commission to see the project through, though it was not published until 1863.

Settembrini is fond of Brunetto, in Thomas Mann's *Magic Mountain* (itself an encyclopaedic work: the inmates of the alpine sanatorium have to find some way of passing the time before they are released or die, hence the survey of the arts and sciences – some of them, such as psychoanalysis, still nascent – of Europe on the eve of the First World War).

Other Italian encyclopaedias were still imbued with mediaeval piety. Domenico Bandini's *Fons memorabilium universi* (*The Source of Memorable Things in the World*) was composed for those who lacked access to other books – a common aspiration of encyclopaedias. It is divided into five parts, in honour of the five wounds of Christ, organised partly thematically, party alphabetically (as with Vincent, Bartholomew and Thomas de Cantimpré). Part 1 is on God, angels, the soul and hell; Part 2 on the world, astronomy and time; Part 3 on the elements (fire, air, water and the fish that live in it); Part 4 on geography, the creatures that live on earth, and the minerals and precious stones in it; Part 5 is on famous men, the sects of the philosophers, the theological and moral virtues, the sects of the heretics, and famous women.

The Early Modern Era

The early modern period, from the Renaissance to the *Encyclopédie* of Diderot and d'Alembert, showed a gradual swing away from Church control, but no lessening – at least initially – of fascination with the supernatural and the inherited stock of myth and legend. Robert Burton's *Anatomy of Melancholy* contains an early reference to the word 'encyclopaedia': 'Let them have that Encyclopaedian, all the learning in the world.' It is both an analysis ('anatomy') of melancholy, an example of it (it assembles the arts and the sciences and then wonders how on earth they are supposed to be of any help, rather like the dark and brooding angel in Dürer's *Melancholia I* with the instruments of learning scattered all around, pointlessly), and a potential cure (piling on melancholy in this way may help, paradoxically, to alleviate it). At all events, it shows the link between learning and madness. It quotes all the knowledge available, and thus celebrates it, but from the sombre perspective of a melancholia which infects this veritable encyclopaedia of book-learning with a mixture of panic, apathy and grim determination. 'Out of a running wit, an inconstant, unsettled mind, I had a great desire (not able to attain to a superficial skill in any) to have some smattering in all, to be *aliquot in omnibus, nullus in singularis* [a somebody in general knowledge, a nobody in any one subject]', says Burton. 'I have read many books, but to little purpose, for want of good method; I have confusedly tumbled over divers authors in our libraries, with small profit for want of art, order, memory, judgment.' There follows an immense list of all the things in the world he can afford to ignore – 'those ordinary rumours of war, plagues, fires, inundations, thefts, murders, massacres, meteors, comets [...]'. This is similar to the enumerations of all the things of *samsara* from which the mind must free itself in early Buddhist texts: the objects and activities in the world are exhaustively listed, bracketed together, and prefixed by the sign of negation: enlightenment is *not these*. An encyclopaedia is in many ways a guide to what is or is not essential, or salvific. (Giorgio Valla wrote a *De expetendis, et fugiendis rebus opus*, published in 1501 – it was a *Guide to what is to be sought, and what avoided*.) Of course, Burton quite ignores his own advice, and fills his work with wars, plagues and comets.

Other early modern writers were more sanguine about the educational value of such lists, especially if they could be released from their enumerative prison and put to good use in *sermo*, eloquent writing and speech. Erasmus recommended that schoolboys keep notebooks: in one they were to collect 'epithets, idiomatic phrases, figures of speech that they came across in their reading [*copia verborum*]', and in another 'witty sayings, anecdotes, myths, historical incidents of moral interest [*copia rerum*]' (*De copia verborum et rerum*, ch. 7). In the Renaissance there was a tendency, as ever, for scholars to become compilers rather than pioneers of new ideas, though there was also frequently an attempt at systematicity. 'The sixteenth century was the first great age of anthologies and dictionaries, collections and compendia of all sorts, in which extracts from classical writers were made more easily accessible for quotation and reproduction', notes Bolgar. Hence Erasmus's *Adagia* and *Apophthegmata*,

Textor's *Epitheta* and *Officina*, among others. (Ong calls Erasmus 'the most influential collector of commonplace material the Western world has ever seen'.) The *Epitheta* was a huge *copia verborum*, 'a vast rag-bag for the use of intending versifiers', and the *Officina* was the corresponding volume of commonplace material intended to provide *copia rerum* – these 'crude and clumsy' handbooks were nonetheless 'the foundations on which greater things were built'.

Alphabetical order was introduced into Textor, and printing made indexing easier: information retrieval thus became much more user-friendly. This is part of what Ong calls the shift from the aural to the visual: it affected encyclopaedias as well as all similar works of reference. Textor's *Officina* is one of the most beguiling of these collections of commonplaces. 'In its studied pursuit of conspicuously useless detail it rivals even Burton's *Anatomy of Melancholy* or Sterne's *Tristram Shandy*, and in its nose for the bizarre it may compete with Rabelais', says Ong, noting that even Textor is apparently apologetic about the 'zany confusion' of the work. And what Kristeller called the 'boring' side of quotations and commonplaces in Renaissance moral literature is linked to the art of memory and the problem of information storage and retrieval – and can be traced back to 'the primitive oral culture of all mankind'. (Every encyclopaedia is, as the German term puts it, a *Konversationslexikon*, an interface between the written word and the spoken: it is the source of information which will mean you can participate in most sophisticated conversations, even if you may become enthralled in what ever-digressive Coleridge called the 'wilderness of digressions' in his *Table Talk*. This theme is given a comic contemporary twist in A.J. Jacobs' 2004 novel *The Know-It-All: One Man's Quest to Become the Smartest Person in the World.*)

The *Officina* is like a dictionary of quotations and Ong gives the first entries under which Textor organises his materials, taken from classical antiquity. The reader finds first of all a list of suicides, then:

> parricides, drowned persons, those who have given their names to bodies of water by being drowned in them, persons killed or dismembered by horses, persons killed by the fall of horses, those killed by serpents, those killed by boars, those killed by lions, those killed by dogs, killed by other beasts, individuals struck by lightning, dead from hanging and crucifixion, dead from thirst and hunger, consumed by fire, persons cast off precipices, dead from falling staircases, people swallowed up by the earth, individuals done away with by poison, victims of sudden death [...] dead from joy and laughter, dead from too much food and drink.

Textor lists all the examples he has read of, including for instance all the suicides of classical antiquity that he could find, followed usually by circumstantial detail, references and quotations. One also finds sequences such as the following: 'trainers of monsters and wild beasts, the four elements, sycophants, buffoons, parasites, fat and thin men, famous and memorable gardens, public criers, sleepy people (*somnolentes*), fullers, the columns of Hercules' (99). There are 'catch-all headings, such as "those famous for various things"'. The eccentric nature of these categories is startling (but not really any more so than the categories of Wikipedia), and Textor has other sections on men who smelt bad, various types of haircut, arguments drawn from the impossible, different kinds of excrement, descriptions of a long time, and a list of various types of worms. The *Epitheta* turns an encyclopaedia into a thesaurus: in order to avoid repetition in speech or writing, you need to know something about the 'headword' you wish to avoid repeating. To avoid repeating 'Paris', as Pascal notes, you can always call it 'the capital of France', but you need the (encyclopaedic) information that Paris is indeed the capital of France. The *Epitheta* is full of the perverse fascination of epithetical superfetation: it gives standard qualifiers and near synonyms, so that, as Ong points out, Achilles is given forty-eight epithets – the Latin for 'tireless, untamed, trusted, furious', etc. Africa is 'glowing, fertile, full of fords, bristling, teeming with wild beasts'. The Arabs are 'rich in odours, palm-bearing, incense-collecting, tender, Oriental, wealthy, ardent, opulent', and so on. 'One thinks of Othello's dying declamation full of Arabia, wealth, odours, gums, and tender feelings [...] One could find here the accoutrements and often the substance of thousands of poems of Western Europe through the Renaissance and indefinitely later.' Ong generalises out from Textor: Greeks and Romans compiled and studied commonplace material (Aristotle's *Topika* and several works by Cicero) and produced vaguely encyclopaedic works (Pliny), while it was the Middle Ages that collected excerpts and *florilegia* – the *Speculum* of Vincent of Beauvais, as we have seen, consists mainly of excerpts from other writers. Modern cultures emerging from oral into print and electronic culture, such as (at the time when Ong was writing) Nigeria, have devoted much energy to collecting in print such things as proverbs.

Alphabetisation in the indexes to Textor was rather haphazard: by first letter only. And he put Apollo first, even though this was out of order, because it was fitting that he as patron of poetry should preside over a collection of epithets for writing poetry.

Another huge compilation of commonplaces, the *Theatrum humanae vitae (Theatre of Human Life)* by Theodor Zwinger the Elder (1533–88), brings together excerpts on historical matters – he calls it the work of 'historian-rhapsodists' from the Greek *rhapsoidein* (to stitch together), since epic poets in the oral tradition stitched their performances together from the store of commonplaces. He uses Ramist charts, which from page to page are cross-referenced by asterisks or daggers. It all gets out of hand, though it manifests a desire for tidiness akin to the method of Descartes and system of the *Encyclopédie.*

Today, commonplace collections are peripheral, says Ong, 'being restricted largely to dictionaries of jokes and of quotations compiled basically for desperate after-dinner speakers rather than for the serious playwrights, teachers, scholars, and scientists for whom Renaissance collections (and earlier collections) were typically prepared'. (But Ong was writing before Wikipedia, before the Web.) Textor and Zwinger are more similar to Homer than might seem: Homer and other oral poets are also 'encyclopaedists, the repositories for the culture's noetic store which they retrieve and organise by "weaving"'.

Such commonplace collections led not only out to 'literature' but back to the encyclopaedias. The *Cambridge History of Renaissance Philosophy*, discussing Calvinist metaphysics, states: 'In the works of authors like Clemens Timpler of Heidelberg and Steinfurt, Bartolomaeus Keckermann of Heidelberg and Danzig, and Johann Heinrich Alsted of Herborn there appeared a new, unified vision of the encyclopaedia of the scientific disciplines in which ontology had the role of assigning to each of the particular sciences its proper domain.' The 'random' knowledge assembled by centuries of compilation and, increasingly, experiment, was to be sorted out. Francis Bacon viewed natural history, the register of matters of observed natural fact, as the indispensable raw material for the inductive method. He wrote 'histories', in this sense (like the original Greek meaning of *historia*, 'investigation'), of the wind, of life and death, and of the dense and the rare, and, near the end of his life, he was working on his *Sylva Sylvarum: Or A Natural Historie* ('Forest of Forests'), in effect, a collection of collections, a somewhat uncritical miscellany, a forest ready to be cleared.

The last of the great alphabetically arranged Latin-language encyclopaedias was the *Encyclopaedia cursus philosophici* (1630) in seven volumes by the German Protestant theologian, Johann Heinrich Alsted (1588–1638). In his *The New England Mind*, Perry Miller writes of this *Encyclopaedia*: 'It was indeed nothing short of a summary, in sequential and numbered paragraphs, of everything that the mind of European man had yet conceived or discovered. The works of over 500 authors, from Aristotle to James I, were digested and methodized, including those of Aquinas, Scotus, and medieval theology, as also those of medieval science, such as *De Natura Rerum.*' It was influenced by the systematics of Llull and influenced the pedagogical programme of Comenius, with its vision of the right method as being able to bring reliable knowledge to all.

Latin was now quite rapidly being supplanted by individual European vernaculars. There were advantages and disadvantages to this. Positively, it encouraged the development of these vernaculars and the growth of national cultures; negatively, it meant the gradual breakdown of a pan-European culture mediated by Latin (though the 'Republic of Letters' was held together, when not by Latin, by the new common language of scholarship, French). *Le grand dictionnaire historique* (1674) by the French Catholic priest Louis Moréri was in French and alphabetically arranged, as was a work by the French lexicographer Antoine Furetière (1619–88), the *Dictionnaire universel* (published posthumously in Holland, at The Hague and Rotterdam, in 1690, with a preface by Pierre Bayle). The distinction between an encyclopaedia and a dictionary was insecure at this time, with encyclopaedias often containing short lexicographical items that were little more than definitions, and dictionaries launching out into encyclopaedic discussions of their headwords, with many examples containing a quantity of useful information about the world that went far beyond mere definition. Furetière was an Academician who provoked the anger of the French Academy (which was dragging out work on its own *Dictionnaire* of the French language) by issuing in 1675 a prospectus for his own rival opus (which, too, had admittedly occupied forty years of his life). He was expelled from the Academy for 'plagiarism' (of the Academy's dictionary) but his work was eventually hailed as more comprehensive and useful than the Academy's. It was heavily drawn on by the Jesuits, those masters of creative appropriation, in their *Dictionnaire de Trévoux* (1704).

Like any other age, the early modern period knew its share of heroic (or tenacious) enterprises that were fated never to be completed. Here is one encyclopaedia (the eleventh edition of the *Britannica*) commenting eloquently on one of its doomed forebears:

> Jean de Magnon, historiographer to the king of France, undertook to write an encyclopaedia in French heroic verse, which was to fill ten volumes of 20,000 lines each, and to render libraries merely a useless ornament. But he did not live to finish it, as he was killed at night by robbers on the Pont Neuf in Paris, in April 1662. The part he left was printed as *La Science universelle*, Paris, 1663, fol., 348 pages, – 10 books containing about 11,000 lines. They begin with the nature of God, and end with the history of the fall of man. His verses, say Chaudon and Delandine, are perhaps the most nerveless, incorrect, obscure and flat in French poetry; yet the author had been the friend of Molière, and had acted with him in comedy (article on 'Encyclopaedias').

France and Germany were not the only European countries in which the making of encyclopaedias flourished. In 1689, the Paduan Pivati, pragmatic and empirical, produced his *Dizionario poligrafico*. Here is the entry on '*fossile*' in Volume IV:

> There is found in various places a type of fossil that has greatly pricked the curiosity of the best physicists and naturalists for many years. This type consists of petrified fish found in places most remote from the sea, and on the summits of mountains; of elephants' teeth and animal bones that are found only in southern countries, buried deep in earth in southern climes, and in holes even in the centre of the deepest rocky caves. Some claim that they are really shells; but the shells that are found underground are in every respect perfectly similar to sea shells, in form, substance, size etc., and in fact they are the same. [...] Nobody, however, has explained this better than Woodward in his *Natural History of the Earth* (1704) [...] He claims

> that, the whole mass of the earth having been loosened [*disciolta*] by the waters of the flood, a new mass was then formed within these same waters, composed of various strata of earthy material, which was swimming in this fluid, and these strata settled on top of each other gradually, in accordance with their diverse weights.

Traditional ideas are subjected to scepticism. Here is the entry on 'Magic', in Volume VI:

> Scoto Inglese [i.e. Duns Scotus] correctly proved that all the effects attributed to magic are mere illusions, and that the spells of wizards [*maghi*] are nothing but tricks and frauds to mislead the ignorant and superstitious vulgar. The theologians then maintain that wizards exercise a kind of control over demons, that they can summon them up, and force nature to obey them.

Many encyclopaedic works were, of course, still being produced by churchmen, both Catholic and Protestant. But this did not in itself guarantee orthodoxy. As we have seen with Burton, the explosion of information made available by print and the absence of a generally accepted method for sorting and evaluating it, after the decline of the great mediaeval *summae* (though these continued to set the agenda in many Catholic countries), could lead not to a sense of knowledge building up cumulatively to a great synthesis, but to a feeling of impotent scepticism, a mistrust of individual items of information (what authority did anyone have for making claims about unicorns, angels, or, of grimmer purport, witches?) and a questioning of the overall meaning of information as a whole. What use was any canon of book-learning in an age when different canons of knowledge contradicted each other – Catholic versus Protestant, Christian versus Muslim, European versus Chinese – and when whole branches of knowledge were rapidly being made obsolete by the discovery of new worlds? In 1692, in Rotterdam, Pierre Bayle (1647–1706) published an octavo book called *Projet et fragments d'un dictionnaire critique* as an example of the kind of book he would like to write. 'I have come up with the idea of compiling the biggest collection I can make of the errors to be found in Dictionaries.' In other words, he wished to produce an encyclopaedia denouncing the errors and inadequacies of previous reference works. But he decided that such a work would not win enough public approval and would merely gather dust in bookshops: hence his plan for a more extended *Dictionnaire historique et critique* that would combine facts with philosophical commentary. This was published in 1697. In it, he showed how the scientific revolution of the previous forty years had revolutionised contemporary thought. His work was *critical* as well as cumulative. It was duly denounced by the French Reformed Church of Rotterdam, where Bayle (a Calvinist, albeit of a robustly independent mind) had sought refuge from Catholic France, and by the French Roman Catholic Church. For perhaps the first time, Bayle's work bore the *stylistic* mark of State and Church repression: it adopted an indirect, ironic, almost teasing format, which turned a reference work into a whirlpool of allusion, cross-reference, subversive footnoting and ever-expanding digressions that had a major influence on the *Encyclopédie*. In Bayle's *Dictionnaire*, the articles are mere pretexts: they set out what is already known, as in a traditional encyclopaedic work (albeit from an often rather strange perspective), while the great mass of the work consists of quotations, anecdotes, digressions, commentaries, and scholarly annotations that gradually dissolve or undermine the constative aspects of the information that has been included. Scripture is quoted – but largely to bring out its absurdities and contradictions and, especially, to play with the obscene stories found in the Old Testament. The destructive impact of Bayle's work, shooting down authoritarian orthodoxies, was in the service of a more constructive promotion of toleration. He used knowledge against itself in order to promote fideism, the doctrine (or feeling) that faith alone can take us beyond the warring schools of seventeenth-century philosophy and theology. (Faith alone, in particular, can give us some insight into the mysteries of radical evil, a darkness that mere knowledge cannot illuminate.) Though Bayle never gave up on the idea that encyclopaedic knowledge could be useful (if only as a springboard for the *salto mortale* of faith), he circumscribed its real effectiveness. In so doing, he was at one with the common sentiment in France (still in thrall to Augustinian mistrust of the *libido sciendi*) that 'book-learning' was of only limited value for the *honnête homme*. Molière's *Le Bourgeois gentilhomme* attempts to learn everything necessary to make him such an *honnête homme*: his attempts are mocked by the snobbish courtiers and dim tutors around him, their own 'knowledge' is held up for ridicule, he indiscriminatingly learns the lessons they self-servingly purvey and is slowly but surely drawn into madness. (Germany, with its indulgence towards pedants and its less polished courtly culture, was more generously disposed towards the idea of the virtues of the *polyhistor*, the man who could know about 'everything'.)

Modern Times
The *Encyclopédie*

The first volume of the great French *Encyclopédie* edited by Diderot and D'Alembert, starting with the letter 'A', was published in June 1751; Volume 17 came out in December 1765, and ended with Zzuéné (what we know as Syene, on the Nile). It included eleven volumes of illustrations, a five-volume supplement, and a two-volume index: 18,000 pages and 20 million words.

Some of the entries betray a certain impatience with the whole idea of compendiousness. This is especially true of the articles by Diderot, who tended to consign the more humdrum entries to the indefatigable Chevalier de Jaucourt. Here is Diderot on a particular plant:

> AGUAXIMA (*Nat. hist. bot.*). Plant of Brazil and the islands of south America. That is all we are told about it; and I would like to ask for whom such descriptions are made. It cannot be for the natives, who in all probability are acquainted with more characteristics of the *aguaxima* than are included in this description, and who do not need to be told that the *aguaxima* grows in their country; it is like telling a French person that the pear tree is a tree that grows in France, in Germany, etc. Neither is it for us; for what does it matter to us that there is in Brazil a tree called *aguaxima*, if all we know of it is its name? Of what use is this name? It leaves the ignorant just as they are; it teaches the others nothing: so if I happen to mention this plant, and several others that are not clearly characterised, it is out of condescension for certain readers, who prefer to find nothing in a Dictionary article, or even to find some stupid remark there, than to find no article at all.

The headwords of lengthier articles are followed by their place in a classification derived largely from Francis Bacon. Thus we find: 'SOUL: Encyclopaedic order. Understanding [*Entendement*]. Reason. Philosophy or Science of Spirits, of God, of Angels, of the Soul.' 'ANIMAL: Encyclopaedic order. Understanding. Reason. Philosophy or science. Science of nature. Zoology. Animal.' 'ART: Encyclopaedic order. Understanding. Memory. History of nature. History of nature put to use [*nature employée*]. Art.' 'CAUCASUS: Mythology and Geography' – myth because of Prometheus, but also because Diderot attaches some sardonic remarks about Christianity, quite irrelevant, but in keeping with the *Encyclopédie*'s sustained assault on orthodox belief, as found in this article: 'BELIEF [*CROIRE*]: This means to be convinced of the truth of a fact or a proposition, either because you have not taken the trouble to investigate it, or because you have not investigated it properly, or because you have investigated it properly. Only in the latter case can assent be firm and satisfactory. […] *See* CREDULITY, FAITH.' The cross-reference, subversive like so many of those in the work, brings us to: 'CREDULITY is a weakness of mind which leads you to give your assent, either to propositions, or to facts, before having weighed up the evidence for them.'

It is not only the cross-references that kept the censors on their toes: the vitriol is sometimes applied liberally and directly.

> JESUIT: […] Read the work entitled the *Assertions*, and published this year 1762, by decree of the Parlement of Paris, and shudder at the horrors retailed [*débitées*] by the theologians of this society since its origin, on simony, blasphemy, sacrilege, magic, irreligion, astrology, indecency, fornication, pederasty, perjury, falsehood, lying, the direction of intention, false witness, the corruption of judges, theft, occult compensation, homicide, suicide, prostitution, and regicide; a bundle of opinions which […] openly attack the most sacred principles, tend to destroy natural law, to cast doubt on human faith, to break all the bonds of civil society by authorising the infraction of its laws; to stifle all sense of humanity among men, to reduce to nought royal authority, to bring disquiet and desolation to empires by teaching regicide, to overturn the foundations of revelation, and to replace Christianity with superstitions of every kind.

This invective is worthy of Gibbon, though without his ironic restraint. The *Encyclopédie* aimed to 'change the common order of thinking': its revolutionary implications meant that, for the next century, most European encyclopaedias retreated to more traditionally 'encyclopaedic' tasks and modes of presentation.

The Origins of the *Encyclopaedia Britannica*

The first edition of what is still *the* traditional print encyclopaedia in much of the English-speaking world was the creation of three citizens of Edinburgh: Andrew Bell, Colin Macfarquhar and William Smellie. The first two were in charge of the financial side of the business, such as finding subscribers. Smellie was responsible for the actual writing and editing. He was the most striking of the trio: a diminutive man with a huge nose which he liked to supplement by an enormous proboscis of papier mâché; a heavy drinker of whisky, a roisterer and a scholar of some distinction who won a prize for his edition of Terence, published anti-Linnaean tracts on the sex of plants, and was a co-founder of the Newtonian Society, one of Edinburgh's many bodies to foster a taste for learning among the young. From the start, the encyclopaedia they planned was to be a riposte to the French *Encyclopédie*: instead of the atomistic disorder of the latter, theirs would have longer and more unified articles, and would be more systematic. They did the rounds of Edinburgh, drumming up interest and gathering together a 'Society of Gentlemen' whose subscriptions would fund the endeavour. The work came out in periodical numbers that were then published as volumes, with the first ('Aa' to 'Bzo') coming out in 1769 and the last ('Macao' to 'Zyglophyllum') in 1771: 2,659 quarto pages in total, to which Bell had added 160 copperplate engravings – all to be had for £12.

Smellie's preface set out the work's aims:

> To diffuse the knowledge of Science, is the professed design of the following work. What methods, it may be asked, have the compilers employed to accomplish this design? Not to mention original articles, they have had recourse to the best books upon almost every subject, extracted the useful parts, and rejected whatever appeared trifling or less interesting.

The works on which the authors drew included over 150 sources: previous dictionaries and encyclopaedias (Chambers' *Universal Dictionary of Arts and Sciences*); the essays of Francis Bacon (a perhaps curious choice, given Bacon's idiosyncracies), Hume, Locke, and Voltaire; the philosophical works of John Balfour, and a variety of journals, periodicals, magazines and textbooks.

The preface continues:

> Instead of dismembering the Sciences, by attempting to treat them intelligibly under a multitude of technical terms, they have digested the principles of every Science in the form of systems or distinct treatises, and explained the terms as they occur in the order of the alphabet, with reference to the Sciences in which they belong.

This may seem confusing, and the preface betrays the anxieties and contradictions that bedevil every encyclopaedic project. The French (usually so theoretical and, since Descartes, 'methodical', to Anglo-Saxon eyes) had produced an encyclopaedia that hacked at the body of the sciences, like the bad butcher in Plato: the *Britannica* has instead digested the essence of the texts which it has fed on. And yet, this attempt to respect the integrity of the sciences was still undermined by the alphabet, that essentially pulverising arrangement: the encyclopaedia was subtitled a 'dictionary' and could not escape the disintegrative trends that this implied. The *Britannica* was, however, to be less of a mere ready-reckoner of knowledge than earlier encyclopaedias. It was to be a tool for the self-taught, appealing beyond a narrow circle of the already educated.

> It is well if a man be capable of comprehending the principles and relations of the different parts of science, when laid before him in one interrupted chain. But where is the man who can learn the principles of any science from a Dictionary compiled upon the plan hitherto adopted? We

will, however, venture to affirm, that any man of ordinary parts, may, if he chuses, learn the principles of Agriculture, of Astronomy, of Botany, of Chemistry, etc., etc., from the ENCYCLOPAEDIA BRITANNICA.

Encyclopaedias are monuments to transience. Before long, a second edition was mooted: its editor was James Tytler, an abridger and compiler, a failed pharmacist and hack scientific writer, who drank heavily but self-published his sceptically inclined *Essays on the Most Important Subjects of Natural and Revealed Religion*. He was duly hauled from Holyrood Palace, at the time a debtors' sanctuary, by Bell and Macfarquhar, and set to work on revising and enlarging the *Britannica*. Tytler was fascinated by flying, and built a fire balloon that rose 350 feet into the air above Comely Gardens in Edinburgh, sailed along for about half a mile, and then dropped from the skies into a pile of rubbish. Further attempts also failed, as did attempts to rouse the citizens of Scotland to demand more equitable representation for themselves in Parliament: this led to his banishment. He sailed to America and lived in Salem, Massachusetts. He continued to carouse, and after one drunken evening with friends, in January 1805, fell into a ditch, caught a cold and died. Nonetheless, the idea that the *Britannica* would need regularly updating – in the form of new editions, supplements (and, in the twentieth century, Year Books) – was now firmly entrenched. The third edition was duly published in 1797 – now in eighteen volumes, dedicated to George III, with a preface respectfully noting the existence of the rival Chambers' *Cyclopaedia* (but putting it in its place as one of several 'mere dictionaries'). The article on 'America', eighteen pages in the second edition, had grown to eighty. Thrilled by this accolade, America responded by pirating the encyclopaedia. One Thomas Dobson, an enterprising printer from Philadelphia, had several too parochially British sections rewritten to reflect American interests and was thus fully justified in issuing his set (from 1790) as 'The First American Edition, In Eighteen Volumes, Greatly Improved'. It was no longer dedicated to George III: its first purchasers included Washington, Jefferson and Hamilton. This began a long history of pirated editions, not only in America but also in Ireland, where Moore's Dublin edition of the work, issued by the bookseller James Moore, was a scrupulously faithful reprint of the Edinburgh third edition, including all the plates.

The Edinburgh third edition soon gained a two-volume supplement, with updated articles ('Chemistry', 'Astronomy', 'Electricity'). This was issued in 1800: Britain was at war with France, and in his dedication to George III, editor George Gleig attacked the French *Encyclopédie*, which 'has been accused, and justly accused, of having disseminated far and wide the seeds of anarchy and atheism. If the *Encyclopaedia Britannica* shall in any degree counteract the tendency of that pestiferous work, even these two volumes will not be wholly unworthy of Your Majesty's attention.' The *Encyclopédie* peddled dangerous ideology; the *Britannica* was a source of information. A strange chiasmus in the relationship between these two great French and British encyclopaedias: sometimes it is the former which knows lots of little things (and is therefore atomistic) and the latter a few big things (holistic); sometimes the former is deemed to have laid one vast and single-minded plot against the crowns and thrones of Europe, where the latter focuses on modest but reliable (and completely un-ideological) information. Which is which depends on the way the Channel winds are blowing (error begins at Dover, or Calais): more interestingly, this slanging match reflects the permanent unease felt within each encyclopaedia about the balance that needs to be maintained between centripetal and centrifugal forces, between commanding ideas (theories, philosophies, paradigms) and the scatter of facts.

The *Britannica* was not without its English-language rivals even in the United Kingdom. The *Encyclopaedia Perthensis* was designed to supersede all others. The title of its 1807 version stated as much:

> The New Encyclopaedia; or, Universal Dictionary of Arts and Sciences. In which the different Sciences and Arts are digested in the Form of distinct Treatises or Systems; Including the Latest Discoveries and Improvements; with the Natural, Civil, Military, and Commercial History, and Biography of Eminent Men, Of All Nations; a Description of All the Countries, Cities, Seas, Rivers, &c. of the Known World. Including also the Whole of Dr Johnson's Dictionary of the English Language. Compiled from Every Source of Domestic and Foreign Literature; and Illustrated with Upwards of Three Hundred and Forty Plates, and A Complete and Accurate Atlas. In Twenty Three Volumes.

Perhaps all encyclopaedias dream of swallowing the dictionary and ingesting the atlas too, in an act of linguistico-geographical appropriation. This encyclopaedia could be very useful to country squires, and anyone literate involved in 'Rural Economy', on which there is a long article, with much practical information:

> When clover is sown in spring upon wheat, the soil, which has lain five or six months without being stirred, is an improper bed for it; and the wheat being in the vigour of growth, overtops it from the beginning. It cannot be sown along with oats, because of the hazard of frost; and when sown as usual among the oats 3 inches high, it is overtopped, and never enjoys free air till the oats be cut.

The *Perthensis*, for all its practicality, is however peculiarly backward-looking in several respects. In its article on 'MART', the encyclopaedia does not so much as mention the advantages to human intercourse of markets internal and external: any so-called 'free market' is not alluded to. Instead, it quotes Hooker on Christ's refusal 'to suffer that the temple should serve for a place of mart'. It also gives excerpts from Shakespeare on 'Syracusan marts and fairs', Raleigh, Temple and Addison.

'The limitation of these public resorts, to such time and place as may be most convenient for the neighbourhood, forms a part of economics, or domestic polity; which, considering the kingdom as a large family, and the king as the master of it, he has clearly a right to dispose and order as he pleases.' 'TO MART' simply adduces three quotations from Shakespeare.

The *Encyclopaedia Metropolitana* was presided over by Coleridge: it now appears as a stately and magnificent galleon, badly holed by the fast-moving lighter vessels of more modern factoid-firing publications. Coleridge despised the alphabetisation of other encyclopaedias, and decided that long scholarly essays would better preserve the coherence of knowledge. Again, despite the authoritative nature of many of the longer entries (the Cabinet Edition had Newman, the future cardinal, on the history of the Christian Church in the first century, Thomas Arnold of Rugby on the history of the Roman Republic and of Roman Literature, James Napier on electro-metallurgy and Robert Hunt on photography), there is a conservative slant that rears its head in unexpected places. Thus we read of 'MALMESBURY, an ancient Borough in Wiltshire, distinguished for its Monastic establishment. An Abbey was founded in it at a very remote but uncertain date, the veracious Annals of which may be assumed without doubt to commence in the VIIth century, under Maldulphus, a Scottish Abbot.' But – more significantly, we are given to surmise – it was also the birthplace of Thomas Hobbes, 'the head of a class of dangerous writers who have employed Metaphysics to the disservice of Revelation; he died in 1679. The *Leviathan*, his most elaborate Work, is now perhaps known to few unless by name' (Vol. XXI, Miscellaneous and Lexicographical, Vol. 8).

A combination of essayistic and alphabetical approaches was often found in later European encyclopaedias, as was a rags-to-riches backstory in their creation. In the late 1850s, a young man from a small township in north-east Spain was earning a rough living as a labourer, helping to demolish the walls of Barcelona. A change of job to that of newspaper delivery boy gave him a glimpse of the world of print; José Espasa Anguera invested his savings in establishing a modest subscription centre for books, and eventually made a long and successful career in publishing, mainly in Catalan. In 1905, at the age of sixty-five, his thoughts turned towards creating a major Spanish encyclopaedia. It was initially issued in weekly instalments, then in volumes. The work grew to huge proportions; in 1925 Espasa é Hijos merged with the publishing house of Calpe and moved to Madrid, under the management of José Ortega y Gasset. The Espasa encyclopaedia is one of the great European encyclopaedias. Its impact on an imaginative young boy is evoked in the preface to *Mapa de la realidad: antología de textos de la Enciclopedia Espasa* (*Map of reality: an anthology of texts from the 'Enciclopedia Espasa'*), Juan José Millás (2005). He remembers the magnificent illustrations, especially those devoted to 'mimicry' in which butterflies' wings were barely distinguishable from the leaves of trees, and where you could see worms that assumed the shape of animal droppings to avoid attracting the attention of their enemies. 'This struck me as too great a humiliation.' He has never visited such perilous and exotic places as those he saw in the pages of the encyclopaedia. His anthology includes the entry on sleep and dreams in various cultures (the articles in this encyclopaedia are short essays rather than a dust of facts). An example:

> In Antiquity, the siesta was considered to be crazy and dangerous, since at that time of day certain demons roam around, such as the noonday demon (Psalm 90:6). To dream of death is interpreted as a marriage in the family, and vice versa; in France and the Palatinate, to dream that your teeth fall out means the death of a relative; in 1697, in Altdorf, they still used ammonites placed under the pillow to have pleasant dreams.

The spread of literacy and the need for quick-and-easy answers to everyday questions of general knowledge meant that the twentieth century witnessed an explosion of one-volume encyclopaedias, some of them delightfully eccentric (or annoyingly irrelevant and biased, for some of their readers). *The Teach Yourself Concise Encyclopaedia of General Knowledge* (1957), prepared under the direction of S. Graham Brade-Birks and Frank Higenbottam, is at first, as it claims, simply a 'modest volume at a modest price', compiled with the help of family and friends. The entries are brief and unexceptional:

> ANTIOCHUS. There were many monarchs in ancient history with this name. Prominent were eleven Syrian rulers of the Seleucid dynasty (312–65 B.C.) who bore this name between 280 and 65 B.C.

A distinctive feature of this encyclopaedia is the sequence of thirty-two blue pages in the middle, telling you where to find further information, arranged in accordance with the Dewey Decimal system so that you can find the relevant books in the right part of your local library. As the reader browses the encyclopaedia entries, she detects perhaps an unusual emphasis on Church matters and a clear Christian point of view. The short article on 'Communism' gives a definition in terms of the 'means of production and distribution', and then notes:

> International Communism to-day links this system with methods of propagation and forms of teaching which are highly objectionable to large numbers of people on moral, ethical and religious grounds [...] See also CAPITALISM

where we read another critique of communism:

> The suppression of personal freedom and the adoption of DIALECTICAL MATERIALISM as the principle of government are the grounds for the opposition of most Christians to modern Communism.

However, Communism is not inevitably incompatible with Christianity. 'The early Christians practised Communism, in the sense that they had all goods common (Acts iv. 32–5).' What a shame that the lesson of the 'early Christians' has not been more taken to heart! On 'Evolution and Antiquity of Man' we read:

> It is a comfort to many religious people to know that there are many men and women, first-class scientists and archaeologists, who have no difficulty in reconciling the findings of biology and archaeology with the teachings of the Church. Very often matters which present great spiritual difficulties to people who have a limited knowledge of archaeology and biology, and perhaps of religion too, are not the slightest stumbling blocks to men and women who have made a deeper study of these matters.

So evolution and Christianity – properly understood – can coexist in peace and amity.

> EXISTENTIALISM. Philosophical interpretation of Man's nature postulating that Man's existence cannot be explained by reason alone, that life's problems cause thinking men mental suffering, and that men must be free to act. Yet the ideas of existentialism are vague.

The authors duly seize their opportunity: 'Existentialism is not necessarily contrary to Christian teaching.' Further on, under 'Psychology': 'The aim of modern psychology is not merely to state how man thinks, feels and acts, but how he can do these things much better and in accordance with the Divine purpose.' Clearly, Christianity is compatible with many aspects of modern science and philosophy – an epistemological panacea, the encyclopaedic religion *par excellence* (as Marx had already noted). But the ideological position of this little encyclopaedia, once registered, is of little interest compared to the quirky weighting of its 'factual' information. The entry on 'Christianity' itself runs to ten short lines, mainly cross-references; the entry on 'Soap' is some six times as long. But even that is dwarfed by the comparatively huge entry on 'Soil-profile', which sprawls across several puzzlingly informative pages.

Part II
Beyond Europe and America

The Muslim World

Encyclopaedic writing in Arabic has generally been subsumed under the Arabic term *adab*, which combines didactic with aesthetic writing – 'polite letters' gives something of the taste of the mixture of 'right practice' and 'correct expression' which the word *adab* incarnates, though its original meaning was 'custom' or 'norm', and in mediaeval times it started to connote the qualities of courtly life. *Adab* arose in pre-Islamic times and celebrated the values of tribal, nomadic societies: an interest in the natural world, a love of animals, the extolling of chivalry and hospitality. Arabic society also drew on cultural influences from outside the *Dar al-Islam*, the Islamic world, which continued to spread: the foundation of Baghdad in 762 provided a melting pot in which diverse traditions could be melded, and the building of the *Bait al-Hikma* (House of Wisdom) in 830 (it would flourish until the city was sacked by the Mongols in 1258) offered a shelter for works of literature, history and philosophy from the Hellenistic world, the Middle East, and far-flung lands such as India. Here, for instance, the Abbasid caliph al-Ma'mun fostered the translation of works from Greek (or the Syriac into which they had already been translated) into Arabic.

Already in pre-Islamic times, Arabic poetry delighted in lists. The relatively lengthy type of poem (100 lines or so) known as the *qasida* would sing of the virtues of a specific tribe. Its opening section, the *nasib*, would describe a deserted encampment and segue into musings on love and loss. A transitional section, the *rahil*, narrated a journey through the desert – an opportunity for the cataloguing of the animals to be found there, notably horses and camels. The final section, the *madih*, focused on the qualities of the tribal community. These virtues were captured in an enumeration of the heroism of the tribe's warriors, the hospitality of desert dwellers, the beauties of its women, the strength of its animals, the taste of its wine, and its daily activities (gambling, horse races, various sports including jousting). It is easy to see how such poetry would eventually lead to encyclopaedic catalogues in which the objects described were, to some extent, freed from tribal context. The *Al-Mu'allaqat* that collected these longer *qasa'id* sometimes contained evocations of animals that would find their way into later bestiaries. Here is the camel described by Tarafah in striking similes:

> Sure-footed, firm-footed, slender as the planks of
> wood in a bier;
> I make her quicken her pace over long-trodden paths,
> varied as a shirt that is striped;
> She can outrun the swiftest camels, even those of the
> noblest stock,
> And her hindlegs race behind her forelegs along the
> beaten path (tr. Robert Irwin, adapted).

Arabic poetry often fell into one of three genres: panegyric, lampoon and elegy, but description (*wasf*) soon started to flourish. The world was seen evaluatively: there was none of the pose of objectivity of modern encyclopaedias, and one thing would often meld into another through metaphor (a form of cross-reference). An animal would be cited for its moral and allegorical values, as in the bestiaries of mediaeval Europe, or evoked to signify nostalgia. In Spain, the eleventh-century writer Ibn Khafajah used an animal peculiar to the Arabian Peninsula to create a mood of longing and to bewail the moral shortcomings of mankind:

> O oryx of Najd, destiny's decrees lead to many a hardship,
> but loyal people are few (tr. Irwin).

With the coming of Islam, there was a need not only to settle the text of the Qu'ran, but also to establish a historical account of the stunning military achievements of early Muslim armies, as in the *Ayyam al-'Arab* (*Battle Days of the Arabs*), based on anecdotes, reports, and the *isnad* ('chain of authority') that set out a list of transmitters for a particular story. In this way, authenticity was established: the same editorial techniques were used to select the most veridical of the *hadith*, the deeds and words of Muhammed.

Once the caliphate and its sophisticated bureaucracy had been established, *adab* started to include advice for rulers and to set out codes of conduct for their scribes and deputies, who needed to know as much as possible about the lands they were now administering. Hence the thirst for information that entailed *adab* becoming 'general knowledge' – of poetry and rhetoric, grammar and philology, the history of both Arabic and non-Arabic cultures. The man who could draw on such a repertoire of information was an *adib*, very close to the *honnête homme* of the court of Louix XIV. At the height of the Abbasid period, the *adib* was at home in both imaginative and factual literature, insofar as these could be distinguished: only later did the polymorphous term *adab* revert to its earlier, more poetic function, and *adab* is nowadays the usual Arabic word for 'literature'.

Arabic writers included many great polymaths, and the Abbasid period saw the flourishing of compilations on a host of individual topics (homes and gardens, women, gatecrashers at parties, jealousy, animals, avarice). Al-Jahiz, for example, compiled anthologies of writings about the latter two of these, animals (*Kitab al-hawayan*) and misers (*Kitab al-bukhala*), as well as a book on the blind and essays on theology, ethnicity, food, speech, envy and other passions. His erudition was often side-tracked by his voracious curiosity into lengthy digressions. An extract from his works shows how the desire to categorise, to make clear distinctions, to evaluate and hierarchise, coexists with the need to incorporate the subject matters of everyday discourse, so long as it was itself pleasingly shaped:

> Discourse, just like people, can be subcategorised. It may be serious or trivial, elegant and fine, or else crude and nasty, either amusing or the opposite. It is all Arabic... As far as I am concerned, no speech on earth is as enjoyable and useful, as elegant and sweet to the ear, as closely linked to sound intellect, as liberating for the tongue, and as beneficial for the improvement of diction as a lengthy process of listening to the way that eloquent, learned, and intelligent Bedouin talk.

Such works, composed by an *adib*, would be used by the *nadim* or nobleman.

One of the most encyclopaedic minds of the Arabic Middle Ages was Ibn Qutaybah (full name Abu Muhammad 'Abd Allāh ibn Muslim ibn Qutaiba ad-Dinawari, 828–889), from Merv in Transoxiana. His *Kitab 'uyun al-akhbar* (variously translated as the 'Book of Springs of Information' or the 'Book of Choice Narratives') purveyed information on many topics, arranged in ten books: on power, war, nobility, character, learning and eloquence, asceticism, friendship, prayers, food, women. But this and other such compilations were firmly rooted within the context of courtly life: it was meant to provide information, but also worldly wisdom and advice, for the class of *littérateurs*. Information was practical – like many other writers of the period, Ibn Qutaybah produced manuals of instructions on etiquette, the art of governing, the rules of bureaucracy, and good writing style.

The *Mafatih al-'Ulum* ('Keys to the Sciences') was compiled in 975–997 by the Persian scholar and statesman al-Khwarizmi. Composed soon after 977, it is in two sections: 'indigenous' knowledge, i.e. that which was traditionally considered to have arisen among Arabs and Muslims (jurisprudence, theology, grammar, secretarial duties, poetry, history) and 'foreign' knowledge (imported from the Hellenistic world: philosophy, logic, medicine, arithmetic, geometry, astronomy, music, mechanics, alchemy). This work is sometimes referred to, erroneously, as the first encyclopaedia, but it has more accurately been hailed as a 'pioneer Arabic encyclopaedia of the sciences'. It was indeed a work of great general scope, an attempt to summarise all the knowledge that an educated man of the time could know in Persia, and it paid special attention to technical terms and their etymology.

The Brethren of Purity (or Sincerity: *Ikhwan al-Safa*: more fully, *Ikhwan al-Safa wa Khullan al-Wafa wa Ahl al-Hamd wa abna al-Majd*, or the 'Brethren of Purity, Loyal Friends, People Worthy of Praise and Sons of Glory') comprised a secret society of ascetically inclined Muslims (hence the 'purity') based (perhaps – nobody is sure) in Basra, Iraq, in the tenth century, at that time the capital of the Abbasid Caliphate. They met regularly, three evenings a month, for discussions on various topics (such as astronomy) and for the celebration of liturgy, which on the third night would – it is claimed – take the form of a philosophical hymn: a 'prayer of Plato', 'the secret psalm of Aristotle', or a 'supplication of Idris' (Idris was 'a man of truth and sincerity' and 'a prophet' according to the Qu'ran (Sura 19), which praises his 'constancy and patience' (Sura 21): Muhammed met him in the fourth heaven on his Night Journey). They were hierarchical, dividing their company into four grades depending on age. They produced what is known as the *Encyclopaedia of the Brethren of Purity* (*Rasa'il Ikhwan al-Safa*) – though the identity of the Brethren is so mysterious (they referred to themselves in the *Rasa'il* as 'sleepers in the cave' hiding away to avoid the calamities that had befallen other followers of the Prophet) that the work has also been ascribed to a 'Hidden Imam' – the sender of the letters sometimes writes in the third person, sometimes the first. A collective work is more probable.

> Know, that among us there are kings, princes, khalifs, sultans, chiefs, ministers, administrators, tax agents, treasurers, officers, chamberlains, notables, nobles, servants of kings and their military supporters. Among us too there are merchants, artisans, agriculturists and stock breeders. There are builders, landowners, the worthy and wealthy, gentlefolk and possessors of many virtues. We also have persons of culture, of science, of piety and of virtue. We have orators, poets, eloquent persons, theologians, grammarians, tellers of tales and purveyors of lore, narrators of traditions, readers, scholars, jurists, judges, magistrates and ecstatics. Among us too there are philosophers, sages, geometers, astronomers, naturalists, physicians, diviners, soothsayers, casters of spells and enchantments, interpreters of dreams, alchemists, astrologers, and many other sorts, too many to mention.
>
> – *Ikhwan al-Safa*, Rasa'il XXI

The work consists of fifty-two letters, divided, like the Brethren themselves, into four sections. The first section is in fourteen letters, on mathematics: arithmetic, geometry, astronomy, geography, music, and elementary logic drawing on Aristotle's *Categories*, *De Interpretatione*, and the *Prior and Posterior Analytics*. The second section is in seventeen letters, on the natural sciences: matter and form, generation and corruption (the influence of Greek terminology is again clear), metallurgy, meteorology, the essence of nature, and the classes of plants and animals. The third part is on 'psychology' – ten letters on the sciences of the soul and the intellect: the nature of the intellect and the intelligible, temporal cycles, love, resurrection, causes and effects, definitions and descriptions. The fourth part devotes eleven letters to theology: religious sects, the virtues of the Brethren of Purity, the true nature of authentic belief, the nature of divine law, politics, and magic. Their encyclopaedia was aimed at the 'perfect man' – part of the universal soul with which it would be, after death, reunited: a pantheistic-emanationist philosophy. The syncretism of their moral beliefs was also evidenced in the way the work attempted to integrate Greek (especially Platonic) thinking with Islam, Hermetic traditions and Gnostic writings. They embraced truth – scattered among the many doctrines they investigated – wherever it could be found, like all good encyclopaedists. They would not:

> shun science, scorn any book, or cling fanatically to any single creed. For [their] own creed encompasses all the others and comprehends all the sciences generally. This creed is the consideration of all existing things, both sensible and intelligible, from beginning to end, whether hidden or overt, manifest or obscure… in so far as they all derive from a single principle, a single cause, a single world, and a single Soul.
>
> – *Ikhwan al-Safa*, Rasa'il IV

But for salvation to be possible, it was first necessary to study wise books and learn all that could be known. The encyclopaedia they had composed could help in the attaining of this goal. It does not claim originality: it is an epitome, but one that is systematic, harmonious – and comprehensive ('a complete account of all things'). It is a summa of what was known at the time, and readily provides references to more specialised treatises. Its influence was extensive, especially in Al-Andalus, where it had a great impact on the Sufi writer Ibn Al-Arabi. It was greatly admired by the Ismailis (and has sometimes been seen as of largely Ismaili inspiration), and missionaries of the sect of the Hashshashin used it when they travelled in Yemen.

Abu al-Qasim Khalaf ibn al-Abbas Al-Zahrawi (936–1013), also known as Abulcasis, was an Andalusian Arab physician. He writes of his *Kitab al-Tasrif Liman 'Ajiza 'an al-Talif* (a 'useful book on medicine' and many other things):

> due to its availability he [the physician reader] need not resort to extensive reading of the various compendiums and the detailed writings from the East. Neither will he be compelled to [consult] the inexplicable words of the ancients, inasmuch as the intellectual benefits thereof cannot be gained save by spending long years at hard study and continuous, strenuous investigations.

His work is in thirty treatises, and covers elements and humours, antidotes to poisons, emetics, enemas, rectal and vaginal suppositories, laxatives, purgatives, fumigations, toothpastes and diets.

Later Arabic encyclopaedias were still being produced by individuals rather than societies. Al-Nuwayri (1272–1332) was a historian and civil servant in Syria and Egypt under the Mamluk Sultanate. His *Nihayat al-arab fi funun al-adab* (*The Aim of the Intelligent in the Art of Letters*) was a celebrated encyclopaedia ('a highly accurate and comprehensive work') in thirty-one volumes (printed edition) and nearly 9,000 pages, and took its author about twenty years to compose. It was in five *funun* or sections, from the singular *fann*, meaning 'class' or 'variety': (1) geography, astronomy, meteorology, chronology, geology; (2) mankind (anatomy, folklore, ethics and politics); (3) zoology; (4) botany; (5) history. This last section is organised into dynasties. The *Dar al-Islam* was well aware of the threat of the Mongols to the east: at this time, the Ilkhanid Mongols were hostile, but the Mongols of the Golden Horde, in Russia and the Ukraine, were allies of the sultanate. Al-Nuwayri had read much about the Mongols, and also had some personal knowledge of them, insofar as such knowledge can be gained from a battle: he was present when they were heavily defeated by the Mamluks at Marj Al-Suffar, south of Damascus, in 1303. In Volume 27 of his encyclopaedia, in the historical section, he devotes about 120 pages to 'the dynasty of Chinggis Khan' and thirty-four pages to the conqueror himself. The account is largely synthesised from two earlier historians, but one passage is not found there. It is:

> As for the beginning of Chinggis Khan's career and his rise to power: it is said that he became an ascetic for a long period, and isolated himself in the mountains. The reason for his asceticism was that he asked one of the Jews: 'What gave Musa [Moses], 'Isa [Jesus] and Muhammad this exalted position, and spread [their] fame?' The Jew said to him: 'Because they loved God and devoted themselves to him, so he rewarded them'. Chinggis Khan said: 'If I love God and devote myself to him, will he reward me?' [The Jew] said: 'Yes, and I tell you more that in our books [it is written] that you [will] have a dynasty which will triumph.' Chinggis Khan then left his iron work or whatever, and became an ascetic. He left his family and tribe, and stayed up in the mountains, and ate permissible things. His fame spread, and a group of his tribe used to come to him on pilgrimage, and he would not speak to them. He signalled them to clap with their hands and they said: 'Let's go, let's go, wise man, spin' (*ya-allah ya-allah, bakhshi dur*). They did this, beat time for him, and he danced. This was his habit and way with those who came to visit him. At the same time, he did not obey any religion, and did not belong to any religious community, but just had love for God, as he claimed. He stayed like this as long as God willed it, and this was his beginning.

The article from which I quote ('Did Chinggis Khan have a Jewish teacher?' by Reuven Amitai) adds that the term *bakhshi* as used in it could mean 'religious teacher', 'scribe', but also 'strolling minstrel', 'magician', 'shaman', and 'quack doctor' –

but originally referred more specifically to a Buddhist lama. Whether or not Chinggis Khan did have a Jewish teacher, this story in Al-Nuwayri's encyclopaedia not only shows the synthetic trend of all such works, bringing together both the attested (what has been found in already-published and authoritative works – most of Chinggis Khan's career) and the new (the story of the Jewish teacher), but also demonstrates the marvellous syncretism of a time in which the same word, *bakhshi*, could mean such discrepant (or are they?) things.

'Al-Suyuti was an Egyptian writer, tutored by a Sufi friend of his father. He was a turbulent figure, active in the theological disputes of the 1460s, who decided that Islam needed revivifying, and proclaimed himself its *mujaddid* or 'renewer'. Placed at the head of a Sufi lodge in Cairo, he was nearly killed in the riot that broke out when he tried to reduce the stipends of the scholars in the local Baybars mosque. He was placed under house arrest on an island in the Nile, where he died. He co-authored a word-by-word commentary on the Qu'ran, but also wrote a history of the caliphs, another volume of Qu'ranic exegesis, and a study of cosmology – over 500 works in all, largely abridgements and anthologies. He produced a significant specialised encyclopaedia on philology, *Al-Muzhir fi 'ulum al-lughah wa anwa'iha* (*The Luminous Work Concerning the Sciences of Language and its Subfields*), covering the history of Arabic, phonetics, semantics and morphology.

After 1500, especially with the slow decline of the Ottoman Empire, the production of major encyclopaedias in the Islamic world started to diminish. During the last fifty years there has been something of a renaissance; there are many contemporary encyclopaedias produced by, or about (sometimes both), the Islamic world. One is the *Encyclopaedia Iranica*, which adopts a somewhat disparaging attitude towards at least one potential rival, seen almost as an agent of Orientalism and Arabism, prone to an over-philological bias. In its 1998 edition it notes that:

> the *Encyclopaedia of Islam*, despite its many merits, does not and perhaps cannot meet the expectations raised by its title. A truly encyclopaedic, comprehensive, scholarly treatment of a subject as vast and complex as 'Islam' is inherently as elusive a goal as would be a project of similar high scholarship on all the peoples, lands, and cultures of 'Christendom'.

It is inadequate in its coverage of Islamic and pre-Islamic Persia and Shi'ism.

> The new *Encyclopaedia of Islam* was apparently begun without much systematic planning, has been published at a snail's pace for decades, and has changed considerably in its scope and implementation over the years.

Its transliteration is eccentric and unhelpful.

> To find information in the new *Encyclopaedia of Islam* on Georgia, for example, one might look under the mediaeval name 'Djurzan', only to be referred to the more recent term 'Gurdjistan' and thence to 'Kurdj' where the article actually appears; even specialists might not think to look first for the capital of the Sudan under 'Khurtum'.

(The *Encyclopaedia of Islam* has responded to these criticisms. There is also, now, an *Islamic Shi'ite Encyclopaedia*.)

The *Iranica*, on the other hand, includes 'a pleasantly surprising number of articles' on 'more generalized topics': bathhouses, children, cinema in Iran (one of the finest bodies of work in film to emerge over the last thirty years), clothing, and conspiracy theories. The latter is a particularly fascinating article for all those inclined to such theories while being aware that they are often the province of those of unbalanced mind. Its author, Ahmad Ashraf, points out that – for understandable historical reasons – the Persians have always been prone to the suspicion that their land and culture are under attack by dark forces. The British, it was rumoured in the days of empire, could cut off the heads of their enemies with cotton. At the end of the eighteenth century, Polish émigrés in Paris attempted to rouse French public opinion against Russia by forging a *Testament of Peter the Great* to spread the belief that the Russians were eager to invade Persia. Such fears seem deeply rooted in the Persian psyche, perhaps because of its dualistic inheritance (Manicheism) that views the world – and Persia in particular – as a permanent battleground between Good and Evil. 'According to the satanic theories [of conspiracy], the failure of Persia to attain its "natural" position of political, military, cultural, and religious superiority is the result of conspiracy by inimical global forces, variously' – how the heart sinks – '"Hellenic westernism", Freemasonry, Zionism, the Bah'ai faith, and even the Shi'ite clergy'. This encyclopaedia does not include the biographies of living persons: it thus avoids the contentiousness that such entries often provoke.

Chinese Encyclopaedias

First, a caveat: the study of 'pre-modern' Chinese reference works is hampered by a bibliographical vagueness which means that date of publication, number of stitched volumes in the work, and even the author's name and the dynasty in which he worked are frequently unknown. Annotations can be haphazard, and classification erratic, at least by more recent criteria. Some works can be found under 'history' when they should be under 'fiction'. Works on medicine are often lumped together with compendia on education, or on language.

In spite of this, it is reasonably well established that China produced what was probably the biggest encyclopaedia ever compiled, the *Wen-hsien ta-ch'eng*, also known in its last edition as the *Yung-le ta-tien* or *Great Dictionary of Yung-le.* We will be returning to it shortly. Discussions of Chinese encyclopaedias frequently focus, dizzyingly, on their vast size. For an outsider, there is something sublime (and vaguely terrifying) about these dry and elegant monstrosities.

Just as Arabic encyclopaedias grew from the *adab*, Chinese encyclopaedias, from the Tang dynasty onwards, were *leishu*, writings of many categories filled with quotation. In fact, they were often little more than vast assemblages of quotation. Filled with reverence for the past, for its learning and traditions, Confucian scholars in particular were reluctant to let any of it go. Chinese encyclopaedias gloried in their size, and their historians revel in the number of characters that went into them.

The *Erh-ya*, probably written by disciples of Confucius (and included as one of the twelve Confucian classics in the Tang dynasty) was divided into nineteen often overlapping categories:

1. Explanations of expressions
2. Definition of concepts
3. Explanation of words
4. Degrees of relationship
5. Buildings
6. Utensils
7. Music
8. Heaven
9. Earth
10. Hills
11. Mountains
12. Water
13. Grasses
14. Trees
15. Insects
16. Fish
17. Birds
18. Quadrupeds
19. Domestic animals.

During the Song dynasty (960–1279), the literati started to classify the notes that they kept: these are the *biji*, or 'notes traced by the brush', a casual name for work that often grew to huge proportions.

As so often, not all Chinese 'encyclopaedic' works were encyclopaedias in any modern sense. Historical works would often include information not just about exemplary rulers to be imitated, but about more general matters of importance in governing the state: in this country ruled so much by precedent, histories and encyclopaedias overlapped. Sima Qian's *Shiji* (*Records of the Historian*) was the first official history of China, in 130 chapters, from the legendary Yellow Emperor up to Sima Qian's own day (he died in c.90 BC). It is divided into five sections: Imperial Annals (the acts of the emperors); Chronological Tables (the kings of the different states of China before it was unified under Shih Huang Di, and the aristocracy of the Han dynasty); Treatises; Hereditary Houses (the major feudal families); and Memoirs. The Treatises are sustained essays on subjects essential to the art of government: rites, music and bells ('harmony and measurements'), the calendar, astronomy, religious sacrifice ('the sacrifices to heaven and earth'), the Yellow River and other rivers and canals, and 'equalisation', more specifically 'equalisation of agronomical matters'. Here is the translation (by Burton Watson) of part of the sixth treatise, on the sacrifice of heaven and earth:

> When the First Emperor (r. 246/221–210) was ascending Mount Tai he encountered a violent wind and rain storm halfway up the slope and had to stop for a while under large trees. The Confucian scholars, who had been dismissed and were not allowed to take part in the ritual of the *feng* sacrifice to Heaven, hearing of the emperor's encounter with the storm, promptly used it as a basis to speak ill of him. The First Emperor then proceeded east on his journey as far as the borders of the sea, stopping along the way to

> perform rituals and sacrifices to the various mountains and great rivers and to the Eight Spirits, and searching for immortal spirits such as Xianmen and his companions. The Eight Spirits appear to have existed from ancient times. Some people say that their worship was begun at the time of the Great Duke, the first lord of the state of Qi at the beginning of the Zhou dynasty. But since the sacrifices were later discontinued, no one knows exactly when they originated. Of the Eight Spirits, the first was called the Lord of Heaven, or Tianzhu; sacrifices to him were offered at the Navel of Heaven. The Navel of Heaven, or Tianqi, is the name of a spring situated at the foot of a mountain in the southern suburbs of the city of Linzi. It is said that the state of Qi takes its name from this place. The second was called Lord of the Land, or Dizhu, and was sacrificed to at Liangfu near Mount Tai. It appears that since Heaven loves the yin, the principle of darkness, it must be worshipped at the foot of a high mountain or on top of a small hill, at a place called an 'altar'; while because Earth honours the yang, the principle of light, the sacrifices to it must always be conducted on a round hill in the midst of a lowland.

Here, stories about the First Emperor are used as the basis for conclusions about the will of Heaven that are still to be observed. The structure of this passage, with its opening out of cross-references (the 'Eight Spirits' are mentioned, so the first of them is named; the place where sacrifices are made to him is the Navel of Heaven, which needs to be located), and its remarkable caution ('appear to have', 'no one knows', 'it is said'), make it seem oddly akin to more recent encyclopaedias.

Lü Buwei was a merchant who rose to become chief minister under Crown Prince Zheng (who later became First Emperor). He was abashed by rival aristocrats who had many men of action under their control, so he copied them:

> At this time in the various states there were many disputants, for example people like Xun Qing [the third great Confucian thinker after Confucius and Mencius], and the books they wrote spread throughout the world. So Lü Buwei made each of his dependants write down what he had learnt, and their combined observations were made into eight surveys, six discussions, and twelve records, more than 200,000 words in all. He thought that this gave a complete account of everything in Heaven and Earth and of matters both ancient and modern, and it was called *The Springs and Autumns of Lü*. It was displayed at the gateway of Xianyang market, and 1,000 *jin* [pieces of metal, perhaps gold] were hung above it. Itinerant scholars and dependants of the rulers of the various states were invited, and anyone of them who could add or subtract a single word was to be given 1,000 *jin*. [tr. Dawson]

The *Huanglan* (*Imperial Anthology*) was compiled on the orders of the emperor in c.AD 220. None of it has survived. The *Bianzhu* (*Stringed Pearls of Literature*) of the beginning of the seventh century is partly extant. The first Chinese encyclopaedia to have been preserved more or less intact is the *Beitang shuchao* (*Extracts from Books*, or *Notes from the Books in the North Room*) by Yu Shinan (558–638), which focused on bureaucratic matters.

The names of subsequent Chinese encyclopaedias are instructive: the *Chuxueji* (*Entry into Learning*) of c.700, and the *Tongdian* (*Comprehensive Statutes*) of about a century later. The latter had nine sections: economics, examinations and degrees, government, rites and ceremonies, music, the army, law, political geography, and national defence, and like many such compilations it was later (in 1273) supplemented by Ma Duanlin's *Wenxian tongkao* (*General Study of the Literary Remains*) – in practice, an institutional history of China (a study deemed by its author to be of equal value with the traditional Confucian classics) that was also a huge encyclopaedia of general knowledge. Supplements were still being published in the twentieth century. The *Tongzhi* (*General Treatises*) of Zheng Qiao was a similar history of China up to the Tang dynasty (618–907), including the discussion of subjects such as philology and phonetics, and tracing (more systematically than before) the genealogy of families and clans. (Leibniz, too, when instructed to compile a history of the house of Wolfenbüttel-Lüneberg, felt that he should go back to the creation of the world, and include a considerable amount of detail on geology, fossils and minerals.)

As with European encyclopaedias, these Chinese compilations often included extended quotations of literary and scientific works that have since been lost in their integral form. This is true of the huge *Taiping yulan* (*Imperially Inspected Anthology of the Taiping Era*, sometimes known as the *Emperor's Mirror*), compiled at the behest of the second Song emperor, Song Taizong, between 977 and 983. It was originally called *Taiping leibian* (*Anthology of the Taiping Era*); its second name was given to it after Taizong read all 1,000 volumes himself (three volumes a day, according to one account by a later Song official). This was the first *leishu* to claim to contain every work in the tradition, and its compilers stated that they had turned over every book in the emperor's library.

The *Four Great Books of the Song Dynasty* (*Song sidashu*) were compiled c.1000 by Li Fang, Wang Qinruo and others, and comprised about 20 million characters. The *Dream Book Brush Talks* or *Dream Pool Essays* (*Mengxi bitan*) of Shen Kuo (1031–95; the book was written c.1088) covered government and court life, examination matters, law, literature, the army, magic and divination, the pure and natural sciences (including the I Ching, Yin and Yang, mathematics, astronomy, irrigation, architecture, etc.), anthropology, archaeology, languages and music (all arranged in hierarchical order). Shen Kuo had been a polymathic government official, and a general in the imperial army, but he was confined to his garden estate when he compiled this work. Wang Yinglin (1223–96) compiled the *Yuhai* (*Sea of Jade*) to help candidates for the civil service examinations: his work was based on the notebooks of quotations that he had studiously amassed as recommended by his teacher Zhen Dexiu and covered the classics, history, philosophy, literature and biography. Each item set out the material in chronological order, from the earliest times to the present.

It was during the Ming dynasty (1368–1644) in particular that emperors such as Taizong and Chengzu fostered encyclopaedic endeavours: in 1403, the latter (the so-called Yongle Emperor, who reigned 1402–24) commanded the compilation of the *Yongle dadian* (*Great Encyclopaedia* – or *Great Canon* – or *Vast Documents of the Yongle Era*). Over 22,937 rolls of manuscript (each one a chapter) – 11,095 volumes (some say 917,480 pages), or some 370 million characters (the count differs) for patient scribes to trace, though in fact the collaborative efforts of thousands of scholars, 147 experts and an alleged number of 2,169 editors meant that the work was finished, almost incredibly, in 1408. It ransacked the whole corpus of Confucian literature, ingesting some works entire, paraphrasing here, excerpting there: history, philosophy, art, science. Up to 8,000 books were copied entire into it. It has been estimated that the assembled manuscripts of the work placed on top of each other would have risen to a height of 250 metres. To consult it, you needed to know the established form of the required headword as it appeared in the dictionaries, according to the pronunciation of the last syllable. There were three manuscript copies, kept in the library of the Forbidden City, but it was never printed (despite agitation for this to be done in 1519). It was corrected in 1562 by over a hundred scholars, who were also commanded to copy out the complete work. The two new copies were stored respectively in Nanjing, the former capital of the Ming dynasty, and in the imperial archives. Soon afterwards, both of these locations were destroyed by fire. In 1644, when Beijing was captured by the Manchus, there was still one copy there: it may have been burnt by European and American troops during the Boxer Rebellion of 1900. Fewer than

400 volumes (some say 800 – which would still be just four per cent of the original) were preserved into modern times.

One of the emperors best known in the West is Kangxi, who reigned for sixty-one years. This man of inexhaustible energies and considerable skill in archery was able, like Napoleon, to bring the most concentrated attention to the minutiae of his empire. He claimed that he could read up to 400 memoranda a day, even in wartime, correcting the scribal errors they contained. He travelled widely through his realms, relying on a small court of aristocratic ladies and eunuchs; he ordered the Yellow River to be dredged and embanked to prevent floods, and repaired the canal that connected it with the Yangtze River; he never raised taxes. He conquered Taiwan and opened four ports of China (including Canton) to foreign trade. The Jesuits (notably Ferdinand Verbiest) flourished at his court: they taught the emperor mathematics, devised cannon for him, and were instrumental in drawing up an atlas of his territories, completed in 1708 as the *Huangyu quanlantu* (a celebrated French work, called the *Nouvel Atlas de la Chine, de la Tartarie chinoise et du Thibet*, was based on it). Kangxi was devoted to learning. In the Nanshufang, a study centre in the Forbidden City, he invited scholars to discuss philosophy and history with him. Again like Napoleon, he was an avowed meritocrat. The civil service examinations were long established – and encyclopaedias comprised the essence of the Confucian syllabus: in 1678, Kangxi inaugurated a new system enabling fifty of the exceptionally able to be appointed to the Hanlin Academy, to work on a history of the Ming dynasty. He commissioned a Chinese dictionary (and a rhyming dictionary of Chinese compound words). He also ordered the compilation of the *Yuanjian leihan*, an encyclopaedia of subject matter, and the enormous *Gujin tushu jicheng* (*Collection of Pictures and Writings*); the latter project was finished after his death, and comprised 10,000 chapters. In 1704–11 the literary encyclopaedia *Peiwen yunfu* was compiled; this was supplemented by the *Yunfu shiyi* (1720).

In 1725, the *Gujin tushu sicheng* (*Complete Collection of Ancient and Modern Illustrations and Books*) was put together by Chen Menglei and Jiang Tingxi: 800,000 pages, 100 million characters, in sixty copies. This is the largest of the great *leishu* to be still in existence. It has 6,109 items in thirty-two sections, under six main headings: heavenly phenomena, geography, human relationships, arts and sciences, literature, and political economy. Chen Menglei had gradually gained access to the prestigious libraries of Beijing: he exhausted his own, then the imperial library, and, after presenting an initial draft to the emperor in 1706, the library of the palace. The emperor insisted that the work be published using moveable copper-types (rather than the old woodblocks). But his successor took a dislike to Chen Menglei, dismissed him, and destroyed all the documents relating to the encyclopaedia's history. (The smaller edition later published in Shanghai in 1884–88 was published by Ernest and Frederic Major, and is therefore known as the *Meicha* edition: unfortunately, it is known to be riddled with errors.)

In 1773–82, the *Siku Quanshu* (*All Books from the Four Treasuries*) by Ji Yun and Lu Xixiong came out, in 2,300,300 pages and 800 million characters, in an edition of seven copies. This may be the largest printed encyclopaedia in the world – there is a searchable edition online.

But – as with Islamic civilisation – China was increasingly exposed to Western influence. By the twentieth century, the vast compilations of dynastic times were still solemnly being republished, but modern Chinese encyclopaedias have begun to follow Western patterns. Thus, as the *Britannica* has announced:

> In 1980, officials of the Greater Encyclopaedia of China Publishing House and Encyclopædia Britannica, Inc., announced an agreement under which the Micropædia of the 15th edition of *Encyclopædia Britannica* would be translated into Chinese for distribution in China. The 10-volume set for this project, *The Concise Encyclopædia Britannica*, was published serially in 1985–86. A 20-volume revised edition,

Encyclopædia Britannica International Chinese Edition, was published in 1999 and substantially revised in 2007.

Indian Encyclopaedias

Indian culture was especially preoccupied by the need to draw up summaries of religious doctrine and moral instruction. There was no clear distinction between epic and didactic. The *Mahabharata*, in which the divine natures of Krishna and Rama are progressively revealed, contains several treatises, and the *Purana*, which focus essentially on ritual and myth, also contain knowledge of a scientific kind. Thus the *Agnipura*, on the various avatars of Vishnu, includes accounts of ritual, war, the martial arts, cosmology, astrology, grammar and poetics, and a long discussion between various characters (including Agni) on religious bathing, how to build a sacrificial pit (*kunda*), the position of the fingers in acts of prayer and worship (the *mudras*), how to venerate various divinities, e.g. Vasudeva, how to consecrate an image, and how to build a temple and tend the images within it. Other topics covered include the world and its regions, the geography of India, astronomy, the expiation for various sins, statecraft, archery, law, medicine, rhetoric, Sanskrit drama, Sanskrit grammar, anatomy and yoga. The good order of the world needs not just to be studied, but to be sustained: *Dharmasastra* sets out the religious laws and the obligations that are incumbent on a householder, as well as offering a summary of the Hindu view of the world.

Jewish Encyclopaedias

Only after Jewish emancipation had spread through Europe from the end of the eighteenth century did Judaism feel a growing need to set out its culture as different from that of the gentiles among whom it lived. The *Jewish Encyclopaedia* of 1901–6 was an attempt to combat anti-Semitism at the time of the Dreyfus Affair; the 1972 *Encyclopaedia Judaica* came into being after the revelations of the Holocaust. It was Nahum Goldman, the last member of the editorial board of the Berlin *Encyclopaedia Judaica*, who suggested a new Jewish encyclopaedia, which incorporated some material from the unfinished Berlin work. The treatment of hallowed themes was sensitive to the wide variations of belief within the Jewish world: the New Criticism was given a voice, so that the entry on the Masorites claims that the text of the Bible was subject to revision – though there is a postscript by Rabbi Louis Rabinowitz noting that for an Orthodox believer the whole of the Torah is a 'unitary document, divinely revealed, and entirely written by Moses (except for possibly the last eight verses recording his death written according to the gemara either in a moment of prophecy or by Yeshua ben Nun' [i.e. Joshua])'. (The authorship of the Five Books of Moses had given Christian theologians many headaches too.) The review in *Time* was approving, and especially excited by the way the Israeli botanist Yehuda Feliks had applied modern genetics, with its awareness of the emergence of recessive genes, to the story of how Jacob had bred monochrome sheep to produce spotted offspring. It also praised the authoritative articles by Arthur Hetzberg on Jewish identity, David Flusser on Jesus, Gershom Scholem on Kabbalah (an eighty-three-page article), the beautiful illustrations, and the 'thousands of examples of the learned, the witty, and the arcane that fill the *Encyclopaedia Judaica*'.

Wikipedia

In a sense, Wikipedia is what Hegelians would call the '*Aufhebung*' of the encyclopaedic ideal – its consummation, its cancellation, and its raising to a higher level. It realises many of the aspirations of earlier encyclopaedias. Their clumsy cross-references are now deft links in hyperspace; their attempts at exhaustiveness are dwarfed by its ever-expanding resources; their increasingly rapid obsolescence is replaced by its ability to police itself and carry out immediate updatings and revisions. Wikipedia is, like the Church according to Protestants, *semper reformanda*: it can be modified wherever failings are found, without being untrue to its vocation (indeed, such modifications *are* its vocation). It even has a history: you can see how any article has grown, track down the omissions that have been filled, the errors that have been rectified, the superfluities that have been eliminated.

At the same time, Wikipedia is a cancellation of the old encyclopaedic ideal. A traditional encyclopaedia, paradoxically, prided itself on its inclusivity, but was *essentially* exclusive. For any item to appear in an encyclopaedia meant that, however trivial, it was somehow notable. It had been selected from among the infinite facts of the world to appear in writing. One problem with Wikipedia is omnivoracity: the distinction between what is important and what is unimportant is insecure. However, this in itself is a trivial problem: the capacity of hyperspace seems to be, for all practical purposes, unlimited. As Wikipedia expands, it is not stealing valuable space from anything that needs it more, in the way that old encyclopaedias sometimes clutter up libraries and homes. A deeper objection to Wikipedia lies in the fact that its hyperlinks to other parts of the Internet threaten to blur the distinction between Wikipedia and the rest of the Web. The whole of the Internet may be seen as a vast, cranky, weird, only partly reliable, but user-friendly (friendly to many different types of user) and infinitely explorable encyclopaedia. The world will be the Web, a celestial emporium of benevolent knowledge.

Part III
A Selective Dictionary of Encyclopaedic Themes

Alphabet

> In nature we find, not words, but only
> the initial letters of words, and if we
> then attempt to read them we find that
> the new so-called words are again
> merely the initial letters of other words.
> (Lichtenberg, J 265, tr. R.J. Hollingdale)

To move from a topic-based to an alphabetical order is to impose on oneself a similar shift in methodology as did Arnold Schoenberg when he adopted the twelve-tone system. A thematic system is rather like tonality. The value (in all senses) of an item is dictated by the place it holds: there can be a sense of narrative or discursive logic, of something unfolding methodically, of a background and a foreground, light and dark, perspective. The alphabet destroys all of this: it is both rigorous and arbitrary (or rather, conventional but relatively indifferent to semantic considerations).

Alphabetical order chops knowledge up into discrete gobbets, tears it out of context and redistributes it at the behest of an order that makes it easy to look things up (so long as you can identify what that is) while making it more difficult to see how any item relates to the others. Of course, in modern encyclopaedias, the fierce uprootings of the alphabetical system are mitigated. Headwords will be set out in alphabetical order, but a thematic order (expository, historical, biographical) will obtain within the article itself. This need not be so: an article on Henry VIII could easily be arranged alphabetically under headwords – adultery, birth, Catholicism (relations with), death (causes of), defender of the faith (granted title by the Pope), etc. But the *reductio ad absurdum* threatens: perhaps, under these subheadings, the sentences should be ordered in alphabetical order of their first word, and the words within each sentence likewise. This would be crazy: the syntax of language (in which words such as 'in', 'heretofore', 'vandal', 'gouty' and 'beheaded' have different functions and cannot generate the desired meaning just by being listed alphabetically) makes such a move implausible. Precisely, the opponents of alphabetical order would say: it wrecks the ordered architecture of the world and leaves us with a heap of fragments. It tries to pull the world into alphabetical pieces in order to see how it is made, but it cannot put the bits together again.

In practice, where does alphabetical order demand a transition to thematic order? Old taxonomies can be broken down, epistemological boundaries transgressed. But new orders are bound to arise.

Schoenberg's twelve-tone system has been hailed as more democratic than traditional harmony. Every note, from C to B, must be used in the tone-row, no chords or modulations are 'illegal' (the reason for which an early piece of his was rejected). The total serialism developed from Webern by Boulez radicalises this breakthrough: every element of music (rhythm, dynamics, orchestration) is treated stochastically, as individual elements, letters in an alphabet to be combined in accordance with new modes of combination and permutation. Alphabetical order has also been deemed (by Ernst Cassirer, for example) to be democratic because none of the entries can claim precedence (though there is a kind of evaluation at work in the sheer size of each entry). Alphabetical order is a round table, with no king at its head. This is one way in which it is close to a dictionary, where the words that begin with the letter 'a' are not in themselves more important or fundamental than those which begin with a 'z'. The total organisation of musical substance can also honour the arbitrariness of the materials on which it is based by turning into aleatory music: randomness and hypercomplexity are mirror images of each other (and the music produced by strenuous organisation may sound very similar to the results of chance).

'Democracy' is perhaps the wrong word for the results of alphabetisation, which can lead to mere flattening and levelling, or (as in the case of serialism or cubism) may be the prelude to new forms of total restructuring.

It took a long time for alphabetical order to become the norm in encyclopaedias. Although both Greeks and Romans were fully aware of the notion of alphabetical order, they did not use it much in their encyclopaedic compilations. The first to do so in Latin was Sextus Pompeius Festus, in the late second century AD, with his *De verborum significatu* (*On the Meaning of Words*). This was the twenty-volume *epitome* (in practice a lexicon) of the earlier work of the same name by Marcus Verrius Flaccus, with comments and revisions. It survives only in fragments. McArthur emphasises how random alphabetical order must have seemed at first – it appears such a 'perverse, disjointed and ultimately meaningless way of ordering material', 'a foolish task to someone who wants to integrate rather than scatter our knowledge'.

Bandini's *Fons memorabilium universi*, though classified thematically, used separate alphabetical orders for more than a quarter of its sections, and the Italian Domenico Nani Mirabelli's *Polyanthea nova* (1503) was arranged in one alphabetical sequence. These were rare exceptions, however: the prejudice against the A–Z survived. Moses Mendelssohn complained that print had created 'alphabetical humans', and alphabetical encyclopaedias have often shown some compunction about their dismemberment of knowledge. (See 'Atomism'.)

In August and September 1977, the US government launched two *Voyager* spacecraft that would head towards Jupiter and Saturn before plunging into the pathless tracks beyond the solar system – perhaps to a planet inhabited by other beings. What had they put into these craft that would inform alien life of our planet and its riches? The answer was a kind of twelve-inch LP made of copper and a record player on which to play it (the aliens would obviously be smart enough to work out how to operate such standard technology). 'This is a present from a small, distant world', said President Jimmy Carter. There was also a hearty greeting from UN Secretary General Kurt Waldheim, and a child saying 'Hello from the children of planet earth'. There was a sequence of sounds both natural (the breathing of whales, the erupting of volcanoes) and human (the noises of trains and trucks, and even people kissing and laughing). There were greetings in many languages, including Sumerian (a kind of secular cosmic *urbi et orbi*...). And there was music: a girls' initiation song from Zaire, a wedding song from Peru, 'Melancholy Blues' sung by Louis Armstrong, Japanese flute music, the Queen of the Night aria (presumably the one with that F in alt) from *The Magic Flute*, and Prelude and Fugue no. 1 in C major, from book I of Bach's *Well-Tempered Clavier*, played by Glenn Gould, with ad-lib humming. (Well, what would *you* have put in? Peter Greenaway's 'One Hundred Objects to Represent the World' was an alternative selection to those represented in the *Voyager* spacecraft.)

Like many messages to the beyond, this was really a message to oneself – a reassuring shop window on the achievements of humanity and the riches of Planet Earth (though without giving away too many details of its extensive mineral deposits). It was the world in brief, a core curriculum, a survey of earth and its inhabitants, a CV, a choice little collection, a *selected works* and a *see also*, a mini-encyclopaedia. There is something poignantly precarious in the very idea, of course, and choosing representative human beings is always going to be a little tendentious (we know a little more about Waldheim now than was generally known in 1977). But there is a more anxious possibility underlying the celebration of difference-in-unity. What if an extraterrestrial race were to pick up the message and decide to pay us a (perfectly peaceful) call – only to find a planet laid waste by nuclear devastation? All that would remain of us would be a twelve-inch copper recording.

Many encyclopaedias have been suffused by the idea that, even if all other knowledge were to perish, they would survive, like an ark, or a bottle with a message adrift on the sea, as the blueprint for civilisation to be reconstructed. What is included in an encyclopaedia is an implicit set of instructions on how to make a culture. However, these instructions – even with the advent of the Internet – represent a tiny fragment of what has been and is known. McArthur points out that we (as *homo sapiens* – we even gave ourselves an identity as *knowing*) have been around for a tiny fraction of our planet's history. What we call 'civilisation' accounts for perhaps five per cent of that time.

> In its turn, the period during which civilized humankind has had recognizably modern reference systems like catalogues, directories, maps, encyclopaedias, and dictionaries, is less than 1%. In terms of the experience of the race, therefore, what we have stored in our libraries and computers today – no matter how solid it seems, no matter how inclined we are to take it for granted – is late, brief and fragile.

The French writer Bourget relates how Maxime Du Camp, the friend of Flaubert, paid a visit to the opticians which made him suddenly aware of his own mortality. Wandering around Paris afterwards, he suddenly realised that this city, too, would one day die, as had ancient Athens, Carthage, Alexandria and Rome. He thereupon decided to write about Paris – to compose 'the book which historians of antiquity did not write about their cities'. He eventually produced the six-volume *Paris: its Organs, its Functions and its Life in the Second Half of the 19th Century*. This encyclopaedic amassing of facts in the face of possible cataclysm attracted the attention of Walter Benjamin, who quoted Bourget's anecdote in his *Passagenwerk*. Benjamin's near contemporary, H.G. Wells, in the essays collected in the *World Brain* published in 1938, the year of the Munich Agreement, also pressed for the creation of an encyclopaedia that would make catastrophe less likely. Believing that history was a race between education and disaster, he suggested that a 'World Encyclopaedia' should comprise

> selections, extracts, quotations, very carefully assembled with the approval of outstanding authorities in each subject, carefully collated and edited and critically presented. It would not be a miscellany, but a concentration, a clarification and a synthesis.

Otto Neurath, who projected an 'Encyclopaedia of Unified Science', appealed to a Darwinian awareness of the sheer profligacy of nature in defending a radically systematic encyclopaedia where a certain amount of overlapping would be inevitable:

> In all this system there is of course some waste, some duplication, some unnecessary writing and publishing. But its parallel is in nature's own proliferation, and no sensible being would restrict one or the other in the cause of economy. Too much is at stake – survival itself, whether it be of life or knowledge. Both must survive, and extravagance in propagation is one way of ensuring this.

From another point of view, however, the encyclopaedia is itself a Flood – a deluge of information that threatens to bring a tsunami of things and facts crashing down onto the heads of human beings. (The images of the 2011 tsunami in Japan were terrifying: the usual boundaries obliterated, a chaos of brightly coloured things torn from their everyday contexts, so that boats came to rest in fields and cars on the roofs of houses, with tiny people wandering around in a daze. For some reason, this dreadful calm after the storm made me think of an encyclopaedia.)

Imagine having to reconstruct a culture from its encyclopaedias alone. Imagine having to rebuild Dublin having no blueprint other than *Ulysses*, as Joyce once jested would be possible.

And if some intelligence came to earth, would we give it an encyclopaedia to read? *Earth: a User's Guide*.

Ark

The encyclopaedia is an ark to save knowledge from the universal flood. The *Britannica*, first edition, contained a nicely speculative article on Noah's Ark:

> It must be observed that besides the place requisite for the beasts and birds, and their provisions, there was room required for Noah to lock up household utensils, the instruments of husbandry, grain and seeds, to sow the earth with after the deluge; for which purpose it was thought that he might spare room in the upper storey for six and thirty cabins, besides a kitchen, a hall, four chambers, and a space about eight and forty cubits in length to walk in.

There was a fine drawing of the great vessel. The second edition of the *Britannica* continued the story, and told how, at about the same time as the building of the Tower of Babel (2247 BC), 'Noah is with great probability supposed to have parted from his rebellious offspring and have led a colony of some of the more tractable into the east and therefore either he or one of his successors to have founded the ancient Chinese monarchy'.

Atomism

The final printed edition of the *Encyclopaedia Britannica* was divided into three parts. There was the *Micropaedia*, a ready-reference section of a recognisable kind, set out in alphabetical order. But there was also, in an attempt to bring together this scattered knowledge in a more coherent way, the *Macropaedia*, still arranged alphabetically but with fewer and weightier headwords ('Matter', 'Light', 'Africa, History of', 'Leonardo da Vinci'). And there was the *Propaedia*, an attempt to figure the interrelationships between all the branches of knowledge: in it, the order and connection of things within subjects would be set out coherently. The *Britannica* noted: 'The *Propaedia* specifically was a reader's version of the circle of learning on which the set had been based and was organized in such a way that a reader might reassemble in meaningful ways material that the accident of alphabetisation had dispersed.'

The world according to French philosophers Deleuze and Guattari is an expressive totality of non-hierarchical entities, becomings, and affects, with no up or down, no inside or outside. (Deleuze saw Hume's radical empiricism as the precursor of such a view.) Here is a characteristic evocation of this world of connections, disconnections, reconnections:

> the real empiricist world unfolds for the first time in its full extension: a world of exteriority, a world in which thought itself is in a fundamental relationship with the Outside, a world in which *there are terms which are real atoms* [my emphasis], and relations that are real external passages – a world in which the conjunction 'and' [*et*] dethrones the interiority of the verb 'is' [*est*], the world of Harlequin, of motley colours [*bigarrures* – the title of an encyclopaedic work of the early modern period] and of non-totalizable fragments in which one communicates through exterior relations.

What a wonderfully superficial world, with its eviscerated ontology! The world as Beaubourg Centre, insides out: a Klein bottle with no interior. Like the Greeks, according to Nietzsche, superficial *out of depth*. And yet the apparently mere accumulation that takes the form of such parataxis is at the basis of Holy Scripture, than which no text can be more profound: how much of the suspense, ethical pathos and striving for a wholeness beyond encyclopaedic totality is found in both the Hebrew Bible and the New Testament in the shape of the little word 'and': *wa* in Hebrew, and *kai* in Greek?

Autodidact

Alasdair MacIntyre, referring to Plato's *Meno* in which a slave is induced into proving for himself the theorem of Pythagoras which he must have understood in a previous life (but was he then remembering it from an even earlier existence?), questions a particular version of education that has come to be associated with the *Britannica* and asks: what do you need to know before you can learn from 'great books'? (*Three Versions*, p. 204)

But encyclopaedias have always been the first port of call for autodidacts. Here is the great scholar Porson, as described by a contemporary:

> For books he had only what his father's cottage supplied – a book or two of arithmetic, John Greenwood's England, Jewell's Apology, and an odd volume of Chambers' Cyclopaedia picked up from a wrecked coaster, and eight or ten volumes of the Universal Magazine.

In the first edition of the *Encyclopaedia Britannica*, William Smellie insisted on a thirty-nine-page treatment of 'Farriery'. He explained, a little paradoxically, that this was because most farriers were illiterate and 'the practice of this useful art has been hitherto almost entirely confined to a set of men who are totally ignorant of anatomy'. But how could the article benefit farriers who could not read it? (*Teach Yourself To Read*...) Maybe Smellie thought that the trickle-down effect would here apply: literate non-farriers would read the article and pass on its useful contents to illiterate farriers. But we here encounter the problem formulated by McIntyre and implicit in the use of the encyclopaedia by those for whom it is a *pis-aller* for more formal education: how will they ever learn how to use it? (The same problem bedevils that most democratic of diffusers of knowledge, Wikipedia: what seems to be free for all is, on several levels, neither free nor for all.) Here are some more autodidacts who have relied on the encyclopaedia. William Chambers writes:

> At from ten to twelve years of age we [i.e. he and his brother] had in a way digested much of the Encyclopaedia Britannica, and by this means alone we acquired a knowledge of physical sciences, not a word of which could have been learned at school. Useful as it proved, such a method of rushing on from book to book is certainly not to be recommended.
>
> – William Chambers, *Story of a Long and Busy Life*, 1882, p. 12

John Stuart Mill worked through the article 'Geometry' in the Edinburgh encyclopaedia and the articles on 'Conic sections' and 'Fluxions' (calculus) in the Britannica – though this is no replacement for a proper school education, he added (J.S. Mill, *Autobiography and literary essays*, in *Collected Works*, Toronto, 1981, I, p. 563).

But, says Coleridge:

> I have observed that great works are now a days bought – not for curiosity, or amor proprius – but under the notion that they contain all the knowledge, a man may ever want (and if he has it on his Shelf, why there it is, as snug as if it

> were in his Brain). This has carried off the Encyclopaedia, – and will continue to do so (letter to Southey, 7/8/1803).
>
> – *Collected letters of Samuel Coleridge Taylor*, vol. 2, Oxford 1956–71, p. 510

And indeed:

> An encyclopaedia appears to me a worthless monster. What Surgeon, or Physician, professed Student of pure and mixed Mathematics, what Chemist, or Architect, would go to an Encyclopaedia for his books? If valuable Treatises exist on these subjects in an Encycl., they are out of their place – an equal hardship on the general Reader, who pays for volumes he cannot read, and on the professed Student of that particular Subject, who must buy a great work which he does not want in order to possess a valuable Treatise, which he might otherwise have had for six or seven Shillings.
>
> – Reported by Harriet Martineau, *Autobiography*, vol. 2, 1877, p. 159

Coleridge remained unable to synthesize vast amounts of information except where it mattered – in his poems ('Xanadu', 'The Rime of the Ancient Mariner').

Another Chambers – Robert Chambers – remembers the day he found the volumes of the *Britannica* in the attic.

> It was a new world for me. I felt a profound thankfulness that such a convenient collection of human knowledge existed, and that here it was spread out like a wellplenished table before us [...] I plunged into it. I roamed through it like a bee. I hardly could be patient enough to read any one article, while so many others remained to be looked into.
>
> – Robert Chambers, *Memoir of Robert Chambers with autobiographic reminiscences of William Chambers*, 1872, p. 61

Biographies

William Smellie, who had composed much of the first edition of the *Encyclopaedia Britannica*, was asked to edit the second. He refused, for two reasons: he was busy translating Buffon's *Natural History of the World* (and translation, then as now, was a highly remunerative activity); but mainly, the Duke of Buccleuch, one of the most distinguished subscribers of the new edition, was insisting that biographies of the living be included in it. Smellie was indignant. How could anyone tell who, of the living, would eventually be worth a place in an encyclopaedia? The Duke of Buccleuch won: the second edition included many biographies.

Why not include biographies of the living in an encyclopaedia? One reason is the need for constant updating: the living are restless, and their annoying habit of doing more things all the time reminded the encyclopaedia of its own provisional nature. Wikipedia has solved this problem: biographies can now be updated easily, and the living can fidget in their shrines.

Boredom

In the second part of the German *Faustbuch*, Mephistopheles and Faust discuss cosmology, travel up to the stars, down to hell, across Germany, and via winged dromedary to Constantinople, Egypt and India. (The account of his travels is a little dry: a list of names and sights copied from the *Weltchronik* of Hartmann Schedel, published the year after Columbus sailed the ocean blue.) Faust eventually rises to the summit of a lofty mountain. The Devil had of course already shown another temptee all the kingdoms of this world. Faust might have expected a similar magnificent and alluring panorama. But his eyes are drawn to a fierce, menacing light. It is the flashing of the sword at the Gates of Eden, barring mankind's return to Paradise.

Goethe's *Faust* has been compared (by David E. Wellbery) to the *Encyclopédie* – not in overall feel, of course, but because 'it is first and foremost a document of staggering erudition, which absorbs within its web of references treatises on magic and witchcraft, historical and art historical knowledge, political history, interpretation of myth, theological speculation, science, technical expertise, and much more' (*New History of German Literature*, p. 548). It is also a *summa stilistica*. But to encyclopaedic learning it adds the narrative thrust of *Streben*. The problem is that, right up until his death, Faust remains unsatisfied: he replaces the encyclopaedia of books with the encyclopaedia of actions (*Taten*), but this is merely what Hegel would call a bad infinity, one thing after another, with neither rhyme nor reason – a nightmarish vision of encyclopaedic pointlessness.

Bridge

The encyclopaedia is a bridge to further knowledge (sometimes, indeed, a *pons asinorum*). It is also an abridgement of matters that can be found in greater detail elsewhere. Francis Bacon, in his 'Advice to Fulke Greville on his studies', discussed the use of abridgements and epitomes.

> I do not deny, but [= that] he that hath such abridgements of all arts shall have a general notion of all kinds of knowledge. But he shall be like a man of many trades, that thrives less than he that seriously follows one. For it is Seneca's rule 'Multum non multa' [Epist. I xxxiii].
>
> It may be objected that knowledge is so infinite, and the writers of every sort of it so tedious [long-winded], as it is reason to allow a man all helps to go the shortest and nearest way. But they that only study abridgements, like men that would visit all places, pass through every place in such post [haste] as they have no time to observe as they

go, or make profit of their travel. [...] Such abridgements may make us know the places where great battles have been fought, and the names of the conquerors and conquered, and will minister arguments of discourse, but cannot breed soundness of judgement, which is the true use of all learning.

Episteme

According to Foucault, every age is underpinned by a grammar of what can be thought and said. Lucien Goldmann comments: 'Insofar as it concretely manifests the archive, the encyclopaedia provides the closest indication of the episteme.' And yet it would be more precise to say that, at least after the Middle Ages, the encyclopaedia is the lexicon of the episteme: it does not, except tentatively, supply us with a syntax.

Error

As he relates in an article in *L'Espresso*, 4 September 2009 (*'Ho sposato Wikipedia?'*), Umberto Eco found several errors in the entry on himself. It was claimed that he had married the daughter of his publisher Valentino Bompiani. He quickly rectified this statement. He was the first of thirteen children? No, that was actually his father. Still, he trusts Wikipedia, but always, as a scholar, checks it against versions in other languages, or against other sites. He admits that not everyone will have such compunctions: and that the vast number of websites on any particular person or subject, even the least notorious, make policing Wikipedia extremely difficult (an entry on a certain 'John Smith' will attract the scrutiny of rather fewer critical eyes than an entry on Napoleon).

Finitude

List, list, o list!

There is a collusion between lists and finitude, as evidenced by the books that started to flood the shelves before the turn of the millennium: their template title was *1001 X You Must Y Before You Die*, where X could be 'films', 'places', 'books', etc. and Y the relevant verb ('see', 'visit', 'read', etc.). Walter Pater was right after all: life is a matter of accumulating peak experiences, and then you die. What purports to turn you on to the wealth of cultural experiences available in this age of aesthetics and tourism ends up sounding oddly *angoissant*: only when you have seen *The Hypothesis of the Stolen Painting*, visited the Mato Grosso (and preferably gone hang-gliding there), and read *Mason and Dixon* will you be allowed to die (and conversely, if you have not done these things, you will not have lived). What a chore! Who wants to live a whole encyclopaedia *written by someone else*?

At the height of the AIDS epidemic, when diagnosis was usually a sentence of death, poignant books were issued for those facing mortality. They included the advice to draw up a list of the things that had made their lives worthwhile. Plutarch, whom Foucault read as he lay dying from the same disease, wrote an essay 'On Tranquillity of Mind'.

> Antipater of Tarsus, on his death-bed reckoning up the good things that had fallen to his lot, did not omit even the fair voyage he had from Cilicia to Athens; so we should not overlook even common and ordinary things, but take some account of them and be grateful that we are live and well and look upon the sun.

There is a risk in embarking on an enterprise such as an encyclopaedia. The projected edifice may never be finished. Francis Bacon's great plan was left incomplete: it was published after his death, as *Sylva Sylvarum*, a dark wood without an exit. Even 'completed' works, with their awareness of the provisional nature of their information and their inevitable partiality and error, can inspire melancholy. Once he had discovered the censorship of the *Encyclopédie* by his own printer, Le Breton, who had surreptitiously cut many of the most subversive entries, Diderot spent the last years of his work in a state of almost unrelieved gloom: the whole thing was a botch of which he could not speak without bitterness.

So the encyclopaedia is a *memento mori*.

(Northrop Frye said that there are two kinds of readers: those who skip lists as being boring, and those who relish them.)

Future

Diderot dedicated the *Encyclopédie* to posterity and to *'l'être qui ne meurt jamais'*. What will future generations think of our encyclopaedias? Too ideologically rigid? Too much in thrall to science, or history, or celebrities? Too fragmentary and sceptical, or too monolithic and dogmatic? (Or some other combination of these terms?)

Google

In the film *Google Me*, Jim Killeen googles his name and sets out to meet the other men across the world who share it. This is a properly encyclopaedic endeavour, both random (names are contingent) and finite (the corpus is limited and all examples can potentially be included). His 'late-night ego surf' becomes life-enhancing. All the people who bear his name form 'a fraternity of strangers': one is an Irish priest, one is a swinger. They are all brought together in Killeen, Texas. There is a US fort nearby: we see tanks, and a rodeo, with cowgirls; we hear their thoughts on

Bush, Iraq, religion (the film-maker is a Scientologist). The film was inspired by Killeen's father's death (we see the scattering of his ashes). Jim's sister suffers from schizophrenia. The side-effects of her medication, clozaril, are given as a side-bar ('see also' – you can Google or Wikipedia it). This unassuming film is an odd symbol of how encyclopaedic browsing can weave you into a personal and indeed poignant web. You are a list of all the Google searches you have ever made.

At the end, the film tells us: 'Take a Risk. Get up from your Computer. Go out the Door. Live Life.' But how to live outside the encyclopaedia?

Headword

What are the headwords of an encyclopaedia? One can always fragment any article into a flurry of headwords and a copiousness of cross-references. Take 'Napoleon': an entry could simply give his dates, maybe include the note that he was 'Emperor of the French', and then have: 'see also: *Eroica Symphony*; meets Goethe; suffered from haemorrhoids; depicted by Tolstoy in *War and Peace*' etc. There is, of course, a natural order of priority which determines what is a significant headword – except that this priority is not really natural at all, but cultural.

Hypochondria

If you are going to die of an illness, the encyclopaedia probably already references it. If you check as many illnesses as possible, at least you may lessen the element of surprise. (Admittedly, new diseases are coming into being all the time: you need to keep checking.)

Many people have resorted, perhaps with tremulous hands, to the pages of an encyclopaedia (or these days to the helpfully illustrated entries in Wikipedia) in order to diagnose their ailments. They have also found practical help: the first edition of the *Britannica* gave a prescription for toothache ('laxatives dissolved in asses' milk') that may have had centuries of experience (or of encyclopaedias) behind it, and advised that both melancholia and the bite of a mad dog could be cured by taking a cold bath.

Coleridge to Southey, 14 August 1803:

> I have been very ill, and in serious dread of a paralytic stroke in my whole left side. Of my disease there now remains no shade of doubt – it is a compleat and almost heartless case of atonic Gout. If you would look at the article 'Medicine' in the Encyl. Brit: Vol. XI. Part I. No 213, p.181, and the first 5 paragraphs of the second column you will read almost the very words, in which before I had seen this article I had described my case to Wordsworth.

The letter continues with a critique of the language used in the encyclopaedia article, which is 'unphilosophically expressed': Coleridge remedies this with a probing analysis of the metaphysical intensity of his own form of 'gout' (*The Portable Coleridge*, p. 288).

Index

Lohenstein's 1689 novel *Arminius* was republished in Leipzig in 1731, with added notes and an index of ancient German customs and general truths about human nature mentioned in the text. Why not treat modern novels as reference works in the same way? (Perec's novel, or 'novels', *Life: A User's Manual*, includes an index.) In other words: what is the difference between a novel (which *refers* to the real world) and a work of reference?

Metaphor

The encyclopaedia can be a mirror, a wood, a labyrinth, a map, a garden of delights. (Like the world itself.)

Mirror

Mirrors can be deluding things: we *recognise* ourselves and our knowledge is reflected back to us. We are at home: even new things can fit easily into this frame.

'The intelligentsia is power's hall of mirrors.'

A popular gimmick sold to the flocks of pilgrims who attended the regular exhibitions of Charlemagne's collection of relics in Aachen in the later Middle Ages was a little mirror that could be held up like a periscope to help them peer over the shoulders of those in front, that the grace would flow from the relics into their eyes and then into their hearts. The mirror was sold by Johannes Gensfleisch. He later made an even more useful invention, and became known by a slightly different name: Johann Gutenberg.

The encyclopaedia has to mirror something. (You? The world?) If we are to trust an encyclopaedia, the information in it must be findable elsewhere: a work of reference needs to reflect (and copy) other texts. An encyclopaedia cannot contain epistemological *hapax legomena*. The encyclopaedia was traditionally a mirror of the world (a *speculum*) – of how it was, of how it should be.

An encyclopaedia was also often a mirror for princes. (The encyclopaedia was a *Cyropaedia*.) Encyclopaedic works were constructed for the bureaucrats of a state administration to use, as in the world of Islam and the Chinese Empire; they could also formulate the desiderata of a wise ruler (and were often dedicated to, or patronised by, a chief or monarch), as in Europe.

By a decree of 13 Ventôse of the Year X (4 March 1802), the consuls of France, one of whom was Bonaparte, ordered the *Institut* to compile a series of reports on knowledge, rather like the one that was to be commissioned from Jean-François Lyotard nearly two centuries later and published as *The Postmodern Condition*. In 1808, five volumes were submitted to Napoleon, who was by now emperor (and a member of the *Institut*, as he would remain): on mathematics (by J.-B. Delambre); on chemistry and the natural sciences (by G. Cuvier); on French literature (by M.-J. Chénier); on ancient history and literature (by B.-J. Dacier); and on the fine arts (by J. Le Breton). The aim of the enterprise was to discover what progress had been made in the arts and sciences since 1789. In some ways, this was congruent with the desire of the state (both the Ancien Régime and the Empire) for statistics, and for a particular focus on the achievements of the *Grande Nation*. But there was also a sense that France was part of the *République des Lettres* and might need in some areas to catch up with work being done elsewhere. The volumes together comprise a mini-encyclopaedia for the emperor, telling him of the country he ruled and its rich heritage. But he could not count on the work to provide him with an entirely flattering reflection. Marie-Joseph Chénier (1764–1811) brought to his survey of French literature the acid pen of a satirist and lifelong *frondeur*. He praised Tacitus as 'the conscience of the human race', 'a tribunal where, in the last resort, oppressed and oppressors are both judged' – not a sentiment likely to appeal to Napoleon, who thought of Tacitus as a sulky senator who took revenge for his discomfitures by libelling the Roman Empire. Chénier's report is divided into chapters: I: Grammar; art of thinking; analysis of the understanding; II: Ethics, Politics and Legislation; III: Rhetoric, literary criticism; IV: Oratory; V: History; VI: Novels (a short history of the novel in France and elsewhere – *Don Quixote* and Richardson ('that great painter of morals, the greatest that England has had') – that is full of tart aperçus (the Abbé Prévôt 'would be greatly read, if he had not written too much') and plot summaries, including a long one of Chateaubriand's romance of the Wild West, *Atala*). He has praised Destutt de Tracy, the inspirer of Stendhal and the leading *Idéologue*, in Chapter I and also lauds Germaine de Staël. Tracy was disliked by Napoleon, who exiled Mme de Staël. Even an encyclopaedic survey of this kind can speak truth to power.

Here is Chénier on Goethe (of whom Napoleon *did* approve – 'voilà un homme!'):

> Among German novelists, it is appropriate to begin with M. Goëthe, whose *Werther* obtained, and still preserves, a success so general and so legitimate. We wish we could say the same about his *Alfred*; but we cannot: this book is too long, even though it has been abridged by its translator. As theatrical supervisor for the Duke of Saxony-Weimar, the author decided that it would be a good thing to proffer countless observations on the art of drama, and even on the art of the actor; most of these are commonplace or pernickety. The only praise that we can find is that M. Goëthe dares to admire Racine and Voltaire, and this is a great deal for a German – though his friend Schiller has severely rebuked him for doing so. Furthermore, a weird and confused plot, an action that sometimes drags and sometimes rushes forward, incidents that come from nowhere, mysteries that remain unexplained, a main character who is supposed to attract our interest but who is nothing but a ridiculous *aventurier*, other characters whom the novelist randomly chucks into his fable, only to get rid of them by acute illnesses here and a suicide there, to reach, willy-nilly, a frigid and vulgar denouement: this is the novel of *Alfred*, an incoherent work in which the talent that inspired *Werther* does not so much as peep out.

Goethe shares the honour of this survey with M. Auguste Lafontaine, Madame de Montolieu and Mme Roche. *Alfred* was probably *Wilhelm Meister*.

Other rulers have been more explicitly re-educated. Shortly after the end of Second World War, it was decided by the victorious powers that Emperor Hirohito should be given tuition in religious matters. D.T. Suzuki gave him a lecture published in English as *The Essence of Buddhism*. In May 1946, the emperor invited a Christian scholar from Tokyo University to lecture to him and the whole imperial family on 'Sin, suffering and pardon': for some time, rumours were rife that Hirohito was about to convert to Catholicism, and he even took the notable first step of exchanging photographs with Pius XII, in 1948.

Objectivity

According to Saint Augustine, Celsus (second century AD), who composed what was probably an encyclopaedia including works on agriculture, law, rhetoric and warfare – of which only the treatise on *Medicine* survives – devoted six books to enumerating the doctrines of a hundred philosophers. He uttered neither praise nor blame, but left evaluation up to the reader. Pliny had shown similar restraint, when he listed the theological opinions of the different schools while not espousing any of them (though he did decide that it was useful for society to believe in the gods). This has become the 'neutral point of view' aimed at by modern encyclopaedias such as Wikipedia: a source of their infuriating blandness – which can usefully provoke the reader into formulating opinions of her own.

Obsolescence

In bygone ages, the knowledge contained in an encyclopaedia had a crystalline stability: it could safely be repeated from one edition to the next, and from encyclopaedia to encyclopaedia. Unicorns roamed the world from Pliny to Vincent of Beauvais and even – albeit with gradually increasing scepticism – thereafter. As encyclopaedias entered modern times, they soon encountered the problem that the knowledge they contained was rapidly being rendered out of date. Some continued to stick to the old stories, and the third edition of the *Britannica* was happy to remind its readers that 'Adam [...] was formed by the Almighty on the sixth day of the Creation. His body was made of the dust of the earth.' Others (such as the *Encyclopédie*) were both powder keg and debris of the epistemological explosion and knew – even hoped – that they would be the victims of their own success. Different methods were adopted to cope with this. One was adopting loose-leaf publishing formats (but these appeared to make knowledge seem too fragile). Supplements and year books were also used to update information: as early as 1753, a two-volume supplement to the seventh edition of Ephraim Chambers' *Cyclopaedia* came out, and this habit spread, as with the *Britannica* or the French *Universalis*. More simply, an increasing number of encyclopaedias came onto the market (one per year, since 1800, at a conservative estimate), each claiming to be more up to date than its predecessors. But the medium of print was always going to be too slow for an age (ours) in which a speaker at a conference will realise that her paper has just been rendered out of date by the one delivered just before it. Charity shops these days are littered with sets of out-of-date encyclopaedias: now we have the Web, which can update itself in the twinkling of an eye. We also know that, as Blumenberg puts it (*Legitimacy of the Modern Age*), we must have but 'provisional relations' with knowledge, a 'transitory reliance' on it – even though we know more than ever before. 'It is easy,' says Blumenberg, 'to imagine this disappointment with the stability of scientific knowledge pushing people towards modes of "having" theoretical propositions that seem less unstable and less taxing because they are hardly falsifiable.'

Ontology

In French, there is no phonetic difference between '*anthologie*' and '*ontologie*': the encyclopaedia aims to survey the whole field of Being, but in fact picks only a few choice blooms. The encyclopaedia can lay out the beings of Being, but it is not clear whether it is the right place to investigate the Being of beings. Abstract entities are generally left out. There are usually only vague and embarrassed entries on justice, or love, or... being. The encyclopaedia prefers, to the unity of Being that speaks through all things, the proliferation of things themselves, even when this effusion of phenomena becomes uncontrollable and menacing.

Plagiarism

Good poets steal. And good students? But the encyclopaedia is *the* work you are not supposed to quote verbatim (though Chinese encyclopaedias were, as we have seen, unabashed recyclopaedias). The encyclopaedia says: 'I am the truth – but don't quote me on this.' You are forced to paraphrase – to resort to the many different ways in which Molière's 'Bourgeois Gentilhomme', M. Jourdain, is taught to ring the variations on a perfectly banal *billet doux*.

Quiz

The quiz is essentially a game in which all the answers can be found in an encyclopaedia or work of reference. Questions that are unlikely to be asked in a quiz are: 'What is your favourite colour?' or 'What was your first kiss like' or 'Why is there something rather than nothing?' or 'What is truth?'

The apparent omniscience of the 'Slumdog Millionaire' in the film of that name has been learned, not from encyclopaedias, but from hardship (what Leopold Bloom calls, in his kindly if clichéd way, 'the university of life').

Salesman

American encyclopaedias employed the hard sell approach. The *American Education Encyclopaedia* had a 'Cease and Desist' order imposed on it in 1938, due to the over-zealous tactics of its vendors. After the war, on 24 February 1947, *Funk and Wagnalls New Standard Encyclopaedia* put an advert in *Life* magazine, after ads for the Parker 51 pen, Listerine antiseptic, and Fisk Safti-Flight Stripe Tyres. 'Here it is again! – With thanks for your tremendous and enthusiastic response to our last announcement! *Please Accept* with our compliments this valuable 512-page Encyclopedia Volume!' This free gift – it transpires – is the first volume of the encyclopaedia: the rest are to be had on a financially advantageous 'book-a-week' plan. And it was well worth the investment. Previous editions had sold over 15 million volumes. The work covered over 52,000 subjects – at least thirty per cent more than some other encyclopaedias that cost up to four times as much – in over 7 million words! With revisions still going to press just before publication, its data was fresh and current, and it was easy to read, both for children and for adults: 'this grand encyclopaedia will be your rainy-evening companion for many years to come'. Among the testimonials, one educator of America's youth, a 'Mrs E.R.E.', spoke on behalf of many: 'As a teacher, I shall have many occasions to use this up-to-the-minute set.' The cover of this number has a black-and-white photo of an attractive 'Texas Coed' sitting barefooted on a tiled roof, her lovely hair blowing in the sunshine.

On the *Britannica*:

> Who that is old enough does not remember the 'campaign' of 1903, the insidious payment by instalments, the sets

> dumped at your door, bookcase and all, on receipt of a guinea, the scholarships, the competition questions, the reply-paid telegrams pursuing you to the innermost sanctuary of your home ('From my bath I curse you', one man wired back!), the 'Going, going, gone' tactics – 'Only five days left and one of them the shortest!' so irrelevant, but so arresting!
>
> – Janet E. Courtney, long-time employee of the *Britannica*, from her book, *Recollected in Tranquillity*, p. 225.

And:

> When too many sleep-starved nights finally got to me, I sold encyclopaedias door to door, a job at which I was surprisingly successful, partly because the *Waverley Encyclopaedia* was the one I had read as a child in Shanghai – I knew it backwards and genuinely believed in it.
>
> – J.G. Ballard, *Miracles of Life*, p. 159

The *Waverley Encyclopaedia of General Information* was published in London in 1930, in ten volumes.

See

'See', says the encyclopaedia: the injunction of all cross-references, and perhaps of all reference.

Sex

There has been a disappointing dearth of encyclopaedias from a feminist point of view, but recent work on feminist epistemology suggests that such an undertaking would reinvigorate the often stuffy world of reference works. A great step forward was made by *A Feminist Dictionary* which includes as examples many tart quotations, e.g. 'Abominable Snowmen of Androcratic Academia', viz., scholars dominated by male-centered traditions (Mary Daly 1978). And: 'DEATH: An important part of the historical experience of women since so much of the actual care of those sick and dying has fallen to women.' Also: 'GREECE: a country with an ancient society which in most histories consists of free and slave men "although women had been involved in all aspects of ancient Greek society, as members of all the Greek schools of philosophy, as teachers, healers, writers, and heads of philosophic academies" (Mary Ritter Beard 1942)'. The entry on DICTIONARY points out how, despite the masculine bias in the OED, Marghanita Laski contributed more than 100,000 citations to the supplement – 'fashion, food, social life, sewing, embroidery, gardening, and cooking'. And on DICTIONARY ON LEGS: 'Metaphor for sterile and moribund ideas and scholarship. Or, the male scholar.' Even apparently gender-neutral entries suddenly spring into sexual life. 'MADRIGAL: Woman's song, an unaccompanied vocal composition, for two or three voices. Probably from Latin *matricalis* (of the womb), *matrix* (womb), *mater* (mother).' (I have checked this etymology, and the best authorities agree that it is correct.)

Smattering

In the foreword to the *Deutsche Enzyklopädie* of Köster and Roos, the objection is made that such reference works put the reader in the position of 'gaining education without being obliged beforehand to work his or her way through the dry deserts of general principles, or the overgrown forest of a coherent system'. It can't be helped: the encyclopaedia is always a short cut. You may reach your destination, but only by air.

Solovki

In the 1920s, the inmates of the Soviet prison camp at Solovki produced a spoof article for their newpaper, *SLON*, on a 'Solovkii Encyclopedia', with black-humorous entries:

> *Prisoner* – person that never pleads guilty. Is staying at Solovki due to a 'misunderstanding'. Has a right to appeal to be released on parole.
>
> *Lecture* – new narcotic treatment for Solovki nationals who suffer from sleep disorder.
>
> *Easter* – outdated tradition of bourgeois-capitalistic epoch. However, it is celebrated – either out of habit or stupidity.

The comedy was risky: one nervous giggle too far, and the already harsh conditions of confinement on this island of exile would be made even more severe. But how curious that the inmates, on this one occasion, chose to express their frustrations, however guardedly, in the form of a parodic encyclopaedia!

Specialisation

Louis Shores, editor-in-chief of *Collier's Encyclopaedia*, in 1962 said that the encyclopaedia was 'one of the few generalising influences in a world of overspecialisation. It serves to recall that knowledge has unity.' There are, of course, many specialist encyclopaedias, but each of them is subtended by this same idea of unity. And yet what if the items that seem peacefully to co-exist in a general encyclopaedia did not belong to the same universe of discourse? We make constellations out of stars that have nothing to do with each other: they are separated by millions of light years, and some of them may no longer even exist. An encyclopaedia is a similar gathering of constellations, and its entries are stars.

Stories

What is an encyclopaedia without its users?

He was brought up in a house where, for long periods, there was little reading material apart from an old medical encyclopaedia and back numbers of *The Watchtower*. Browsing through the first, he convinced himself that he was suffering from every illness in its pages (see HYPOCHONDRIA); the dire and lavishly illustrated warnings in the second convinced him that the world was about to end at any moment, and that he would not be joining the gently smiling people holding hands in a suburban garden surrounded by lambs lying down unafraid next to lions (see APOCALYPSE). Later, when he decided he wanted to be a doctor, the mother of a schoolfriend living two streets up the hill would invite him round to have a look at the *Encyclopaedia Britannica* with its superimposed transparent plates showing the inner organs of the body and their interrelations. Alone in the grey light of the living room, sipping a glass of special formula orange juice, he stared at the lungs and the liver and the spleen and how they were all related. Later still, he read in Richard Hoggart's *The Uses of Literacy* of how, in working-class milieus, there was always someone in the community with an encyclopaedia that he or she was ready to share with neighbours.

Michael Parkinson relates (in the *Guardian* of 4 November 2010) an evening at The Ivy, Covent Garden's celebrated eatery, in the company of Denis Law and George Best. They started arguing about the origins of football, and became so heated that Best stormed out. But half an hour later, 'he reappeared with a huge encyclopaedia under his arm, with which he proved his point'. The encyclopaedia was later spotted in a table in Tramp, the nightclub in Jermyn Street. (After all, James Joyce had boasted that he could bring 'to tavern and to brothel/The mind of witty Aristotle'.)

She suffered from periodic attacks of depression; but, living in Paris, she found that a good pick-me-up and disperser of the blue meanies and the black dog was the purchase of a new volume in the *Que Sais-Je?* series. *Que Sais-Je?* was the motto of Montaigne: 'what do I know?' – the implication being that he was not sure whether he knew anything, but did not want to claim, either, that he knew nothing. This collection, despite its title, is published by the Presses Universitaires de France, and contains volumes on a vast range of more or less knowable subjects – transexualism, the constitutions of France, town planning, pre-Columbian civilisation, Alzheimer's disease... Together they comprise a fine encyclopaedia, in thematic form: one curious feature is that every book is 128 pages long, whether it is on 'Hegel and Hegelianism', 'Fetishism', 'Constantine the Great', or 'Anglo-Saxon Masonic rites'. She found, too, that her lack of confidence with men could partly be overcome with the help of these belated examples of the German *Konversationslexikon*. Getting to know an Irishman was much easier with the *Que Sais-Je?* on 'The Celts' and 'Ireland', a Peruvian who had come to Paris to study (he said this with a perfectly straight face) 'black magic' was impressed by her awareness of the main currents of 'esoteric thought', and an American friend warmed to her knowledge of 'La Country Music'. Even if the friendships faltered, she had still learned a store of useful things.

Theology

We have already seen that the *Encyclopaedia Iranica* is sceptical about the virtues of the *Encyclopaedia of Islam*. The fact that encyclopaedias can attack each other with a certain *odium theologicum* should come as no surprise, for behind the encyclopaedia of every culture lie the sacred texts of that culture. This, at least, used to be the case: the five Confucian classics underlay the encyclopaedias of the Chinese Empire; the Bible was the foundation of post-classical European encyclopaedias until at least the eighteenth century; McArthur has called the Vedas 'an ancient "Encyclopaedia Indica"'. Even in Islam, the Qu'ran, which is a hortatory and expostulative text rather than a catalogue of things, gave birth to a hadith which says: 'The first thing God created was the pen. He created the tablet and said to the pen, "Write!" And the pen answered: "What shall I write?" He said: "Write My knowledge of My creation till the Day of Resurrection."' The *Encyclopaedia of Islam* still questions whether reference should be made to anything outside the *Dar al-Islam*.

The *Concise Encyclopaedia of Islam* notes that Hughes' *Dictionary of Islam* from the nineteenth century 'has a missionary bias that forces Pakistani editions to white-out objectionable passages on almost every page' (ib., p. 262).

Virus

On 30 March 2009, Shane Fitzgerald, of University College, Dublin, added a few words to Maurice Jarre's entry when the latter died. 'One could say my life itself has been one long soundtrack. Music was my life, music brought me to life, and music is how I will be remembered long after I leave this life. When I die there will be a final waltz playing in my head, and that only I can hear...' This was repeated in the *Guardian* obituary of 31 March 2009. It then spread across the world. (I have copied this information from Andrew Dalby, whom I trust. He states also that the footnotes to articles often reference sources that are mirroring Wikipedia itself. Mirror mirrored on mirror is all the show. Instead of the encyclopaedia being a *speculum mundi*, soon the whole world will simply be a mirror of Wikipedia. See MIRROR.)

Zeppelin

French novelist François Bon on the French Wikipedia: 'Our encyclopaedias had been, since childhood, our most precious family and collective possessions.' And: 'I use it to find immediately a point of bibliography, the date of publication of a particular book by Duras, even if I carry out further research elsewhere.' Are other sources any more reliable? But in the offices of publishers, says Bon, it is pages from Google and Wikipedia that are always open on the computers.

Bon is a good example of a writer whose work (and the kind of literary experiment that he encourages) mingles fiction with the kind of facts that can be derived from works of reference. And online fiction can contain hyperlinks of the kind found in Wikipedia (these links disappear, he notes, in the PDF version). Earlier encyclopaedias, he adds, can still provide us with a frisson that goes beyond the provision of information. '*Le Grand Larousse du XIXe siècle* reads like a novel, filled as it is with crimes and horrors.'

Bon is an object as well as a subject in the Wiki-realm. The English-language Wikipedia says of him: 'François Bon loves loud rock music and often writes while listening this kind of music [sic].' The French version is a little more specific, noting his radio programmes devoted to the Rolling Stones and to Led Zeppelin.

'Zeppelin': this seems, at least alphabetically, a good place at which to end.

Biographical note

Andrew Brown is a college dropout and freelance translator from the Black Country. His other works include two 'Brief Lives' for Hesperus Press – *Flaubert* (2009) and *Stendhal* (2010) – as well as a series of prose poems in dialect, *Yoe doe arf goo all round the Wrekin*; a short survey of notable fakes, *Playing in Winter's Sun*; and a satirical study of life after Babel, *The King Is Naked* (forthcoming). He is the founder of the underground association RAGOUT (Revolutionary Anarchist Group of Utopian Translators).

HESPERUS PRESS

Hesperus Press is committed to bringing near what is far – far both in space and time. Works written by the greatest authors, and unjustly neglected or simply little known in the English-speaking world, are made accessible through new translations and a completely fresh editorial approach. Through these classic works, the reader is introduced to the greatest writers from all times and all cultures.

For more information on Hesperus Press, please visit our website: **www.hesperuspress.com**

SELECTED TITLES FROM HESPERUS PRESS

Author	*Title*	*Foreword writer*
Pietro Aretino	*The School of Whoredom*	Paul Bailey
Pietro Aretino	*The Secret Life of Nuns*	
Jane Austen	*Lesley Castle*	Zoë Heller
Jane Austen	*Love and Friendship*	Fay Weldon
Honoré de Balzac	*Colonel Chabert*	A.N. Wilson
Charles Baudelaire	*On Wine and Hashish*	Margaret Drabble
Giovanni Boccaccio	*Life of Dante*	A.N. Wilson
Charlotte Brontë	*The Spell*	
Emily Brontë	*Poems of Solitude*	Helen Dunmore
Mikhail Bulgakov	*Fatal Eggs*	Doris Lessing
Mikhail Bulgakov	*The Heart of a Dog*	A.S. Byatt
Giacomo Casanova	*The Duel*	Tim Parks
Miguel de Cervantes	*The Dialogue of the Dogs*	Ben Okri
Geoffrey Chaucer	*The Parliament of Birds*	
Anton Chekhov	*The Story of a Nobody*	Louis de Bernières
Anton Chekhov	*Three Years*	William Fiennes
Wilkie Collins	*The Frozen Deep*	
Joseph Conrad	*Heart of Darkness*	A.N. Wilson
Joseph Conrad	*The Return*	Colm Tóibín
Gabriele D'Annunzio	*The Book of the Virgins*	Tim Parks
Dante Alighieri	*The Divine Comedy: Inferno*	
Dante Alighieri	*New Life*	Louis de Bernières
Daniel Defoe	*The King of Pirates*	Peter Ackroyd
Marquis de Sade	*Incest*	Janet Street-Porter
Charles Dickens	*The Haunted House*	Peter Ackroyd
Charles Dickens	*A House to Let*	
Fyodor Dostoevsky	*The Double*	Jeremy Dyson
Fyodor Dostoevsky	*Poor People*	Charlotte Hobson
Alexandre Dumas	*One Thousand and One Ghosts*	

George Eliot	*Amos Barton*	Matthew Sweet
Henry Fielding	*Jonathan Wild the Great*	Peter Ackroyd
F. Scott Fitzgerald	*The Popular Girl*	Helen Dunmore
Gustave Flaubert	*Memoirs of a Madman*	Germaine Greer
Ugo Foscolo	*Last Letters of Jacopo Ortis*	Valerio Massimo Manfredi
Elizabeth Gaskell	*Lois the Witch*	Jenny Uglow
Théophile Gautier	*The Jinx*	Gilbert Adair
André Gide	*Theseus*	
Johann Wolfgang von Goethe	*The Man of Fifty*	A.S. Byatt
Nikolai Gogol	*The Squabble*	Patrick McCabe
E.T.A. Hoffmann	*Mademoiselle de Scudéri*	Gilbert Adair
Victor Hugo	*The Last Day of a Condemned Man*	Libby Purves
Joris-Karl Huysmans	*With the Flow*	Simon Callow
Henry James	*In the Cage*	Libby Purves
Franz Kafka	*Metamorphosis*	Martin Jarvis
Franz Kafka	*The Trial*	Zadie Smith
John Keats	*Fugitive Poems*	Andrew Motion
Heinrich von Kleist	*The Marquise of O–*	Andrew Miller
Mikhail Lermontov	*A Hero of Our Time*	Doris Lessing
Nikolai Leskov	*Lady Macbeth of Mtsensk*	Gilbert Adair
Carlo Levi	*Words are Stones*	Anita Desai
Xavier de Maistre	*A Journey Around my Room*	Alain de Botton
André Malraux	*The Way of the Kings*	Rachel Seiffert
Katherine Mansfield	*Prelude*	William Boyd
Edgar Lee Masters	*Spoon River Anthology*	Shena Mackay
Guy de Maupassant	*Butterball*	Germaine Greer
Prosper Mérimée	*Carmen*	Philip Pullman
Sir Thomas More	*The History of King Richard III*	Sister Wendy Beckett
Sándor Petőfi	*John the Valiant*	George Szirtes

Francis Petrarch	*My Secret Book*	Germaine Greer
Luigi Pirandello	*Loveless Love*	
Edgar Allan Poe	*Eureka*	Sir Patrick Moore
Alexander Pope	*The Rape of the Lock* and *A Key to the Lock*	Peter Ackroyd
Antoine-François Prévost	*Manon Lescaut*	Germaine Greer
Marcel Proust	*Pleasures and Days*	A.N. Wilson
Alexander Pushkin	*Dubrovsky*	Patrick Neate
Alexander Pushkin	*Ruslan and Lyudmila*	Colm Tóibín
François Rabelais	*Pantagruel*	Paul Bailey
François Rabelais	*Gargantua*	Paul Bailey
Christina Rossetti	*Commonplace*	Andrew Motion
George Sand	*The Devil's Pool*	Victoria Glendinning
Jean-Paul Sartre	*The Wall*	Justin Cartwright
Friedrich von Schiller	*The Ghost-seer*	Martin Jarvis
Mary Shelley	*Transformation*	
Percy Bysshe Shelley	*Zastrozzi*	Germaine Greer
Stendhal	*Memoirs of an Egotist*	Doris Lessing
Robert Louis Stevenson	*Dr Jekyll and Mr Hyde*	Helen Dunmore
Theodor Storm	*The Lake of the Bees*	Alan Sillitoe
Leo Tolstoy	*The Death of Ivan Ilych*	
Leo Tolstoy	*Hadji Murat*	Colm Tóibín
Ivan Turgenev	*Faust*	Simon Callow
Mark Twain	*The Diary of Adam and Eve*	John Updike
Mark Twain	*Tom Sawyer, Detective*	
Oscar Wilde	*The Portrait of Mr W.H.*	Peter Ackroyd
Virginia Woolf	*Carlyle's House and Other Sketches*	Doris Lessing
Virginia Woolf	*Monday or Tuesday*	Scarlett Thomas
Emile Zola	*For a Night of Love*	A.N. Wilson